A LITTLE COMMONWEALTH

A LITTLE COMMONWEALTH

Family Life in Plymouth Colony

SECOND EDITION

John Demos

OXFORD
UNIVERSITY PRESS
2000

OXFORD

UNIVERSITY PRESS

Oxford   New York

Athens   Auckland   Bangkok   Bogotá   Buenos Aires   Calcutta
Cape Town   Chennai   Dar es Salaam   Delhi   Florence   Hong Kong   Istanbul
Karachi   Kuala Lumpur   Madrid   Melbourne   Mexico City   Mumbai
Nairobi   Paris   São Paulo   Singapore   Taipei   Tokyo   Toronto   Warsaw

and associated companies in

Berlin   Ibadan

Published by Oxford University Press, Inc.
198 Madison Avenue, New York, New York 10016

Oxford is a registered trademark of Oxford University Press.

Library of Congress Cataloging-in-Publication Data
Demos, John.
A little commonwealth : family life in Plymouth Colony / John
Demos. -- 2nd ed.
    p.   cm.
Includes index.
ISBN 0-19-512889-3.   ISBN 0-19-512890-7 (pbk)
    1. Family--Massachusetts--Plymouth. 2. Plymouth (Mass.)--Social
life and customs.   I. Title.
HQ557.P5D4   1999
306.85'0974'82--dc21   99-12551

1 3 5 7 9 8 6 4 2

Printed in the United States of America

For my Mother
and
For the Memory of My Father

FOREWORD

to the Second Edition

❧

Books of history have their own histories. And this one's is more peculiar than most. From doubtful and problematic beginnings, to an unexpectedly wide reception, through a remarkably extended publishing life, it has surprised me again and again. Now, it springs a further surprise: At the venerable age of thirty, it will be reborn in a new edition.

At first, I had no thought of a book at all. A graduate seminar paper (1963) grew modestly into a scholarly article (1965) which, in turn, caught the eye of the staff at Plimoth Plantation (the fine outdoor museum near the site of the famous "Pilgrim" settlement of 1620). Plantation officials then proposed a further stage: to extend the published article into a piece for their pamphlet series on early Plymouth history. The work they envisioned would directly engage the questions of Plantation visitors, around the general topic of "domestic life."

These outward inducements were mixed, of course, with an author's own, more interior, intentions. My initial focus (in the seminar paper) had been the demography of Plymouth families. To that end I had canvassed large heaps of vital records, performed the analytic technique known to scholars as "family reconstitution," and developed my results into a variety of graphs and tables. Though never a skilled practitioner of "quantitative history," I did (and do) recognize the power of numbers to establish a baseline for past experience.

The Plantation, for its part, was centrally concerned with material life: the physical surroundings, the objects, the artifacts. And this sent me off in a very different direction—toward what scholars have come to call "material culture history." I spent most of one summer exploring the Plantation's exhibits, talking with its guides and docents, and learning as best I could from the published work of archaeologists, architectural historians, and experts on such seemingly arcane matters as furniture, clothing, tools, and household crafts. (This was, indeed, the start of a lasting love affair with the "things" of early America, a passion that grips me still.)

Meanwhile, my deepest interest all along was another aspect entirely: the psychology, the whole, many-sided emotional dimension, of family. But I saw this as a particularly difficult challenge. A year of intensive, graduate-level study in psychology, including an extraordinary seminar with the psychoanalyst Erik Erikson, would be needed to prepare me. And Erikson's own writings on "psychohistory" would become both guide and inspiration for my subsequent efforts with Plymouth.

When, at last, I was ready to write, I could only hope that these various approaches might somehow conjoin to make a package. A more immediate problem was their aggregate size. My pile of draft-pages quickly outgrew its "pamphlet" specifications; for better or worse, it would have to be a book. My sponsors at Plimoth Plantation swallowed hard and accepted the change. But their publisher balked. The larger study I was now creating raised new questions of production—and of sale. And when the work was fully done, the publisher declined to take it.

In that dark moment . . . enter a different publisher, Oxford University Press, in the reassuring form of Sheldon Meyer. Sheldon's preeminence among History editors is now widely acknowledged, but both of us were rookies back then. That he was willing to chance it with such a young and untested scholar—peddling such a decidedly unorthodox project—remains for me something of a miracle. But chance it he, and Oxford, did. A contract was offered, and a book produced, on the cusp between succeeding decades.

Publication brought further surprises, all of them gratifying. For one thing, readers would be more numerous and varied than any of us (especially that first, unwilling publisher) had foreseen. Without quite meaning to, I had written a "crossover" book—the kind that might appeal to "generalists" (including students) as well as my fellow scholars. This factor, more than any other, would ensure its in-print longevity.

But, most striking and most important of all was the context in which the book would be received. Almost at once it was lumped with others as part of a new historical mini-genre, which took the name "community studies." The impulse for this lumping was simple enough: Several different works, all published within the space of mere months, seemed to converge in offering detailed portraits of particular early American communities. Though their thematic and methodological emphasis varied, all were joined in privileging depth over breadth, and analysis over narrative description. In the years to follow, community studies would sprout and blossom across a very broad scholarly range. A working conference organized under that rubric at Brandeis University in 1972 produced a truly astonishing response. Eighty-eight different historians, each with a community study in progress (or in prospect), came together to share ideas, experience, and a mutually reinforcing excitement.

In the final event, the stakes were higher still. Suddenly (or so it seemed to me) scholars began to speak of a "new social history"—in which, again, my book could claim some part. The "new" in this case necessarily implied an "old," and the boundary between them was not always clear. But three elements appeared to be central: a strong focus on everyday life and ordinary people; a central role for analysis and interpretation; and a readiness to borrow both theory and method from the social sciences.

As the new currents gathered force, their reach expanded dramatically. From New England to other early American sites. From the colonial to the national period. From social experience to political, or economic, or religious (or what have you) behavior. For a time it was possible to imagine a virtual *imperium* of new scholarship, something that might transform the entire discipline.

Such at least was the prospect envisioned, in giddy moments, by early advocates and practitioners. But, inevitably, questions would arise—and a reaction would set in. The questions were of many sorts. Some embraced method: Clearly, there were difficulties in transferring concepts and research strategies across disciplinary frontiers. Others went to language: As technical terms and phrases proliferated throughout the new histories, their audience shrank to ever smaller groups of specialists. But most troubling of all was the specter of spreading "fragmentation." New studies, however ingenious in conception and sophisticated in technique, seemed endlessly to divide and subdivide the historical landscape. As individual flowers grew tall in their exotic myriads, the garden itself disappeared from view. Increasingly, by the late 1970s, historians as a whole drew back—or paused to take a second look. And, by the early 80s, the momentum of the "new" was clearly spent.

Fast-forward, now, to the late 1990s. Much has changed—in the author, in the overall historical enterprise, in the shape of the Academy. The new social history, like all of its first proponents, has grayed considerably. Shrunken in scope, and shorn of its most excessive claims, it belongs now to the scholarly mainstream. Quantification—to take the most obvious example—is no longer a war whoop in the battle for and against reform. Few would deny its uses here and there, but none would argue for its importance everywhere. Moreover, its interior parts—the details of method and technique—have been substantially refined over the years. In short, quantitative history is both smaller and better than it was before. Psychohistory, meanwhile, has undergone a similar transformation. Its early and often blatantly reductive boasts are heard no more. Yet studies that treat the question of human motive—for instance, biographies—increasingly, even routinely, borrow from psychological theory (and practice). And so, too, with work on material culture. In truth, this last track has been slower to merge with other scholarship; but the process seems, just recently, to have been moving forward with impressive speed.

The author, meanwhile, has changed his own professional stance quite drastically. Though still a believer in rigorously analytic approaches, and though deeply grateful for my previous involvements that way, I have (re)discovered an interest in the historian's ancient practice of narrative. As the new has become old, the old is—for me at least—again new.

And what of the book itself? To be sure, it wears a new jacket; but what of the body that lies underneath? No doubt, some parts could be changed, and possibly a few *should* be changed. It is undeniably tempting to trim and tuck, to add and subtract, in response to developing scholarly fashions—or even to some apparent advance-in-knowledge. For all that, I have chosen to let the work stand as I wrote it three decades ago. Books, I think, have a kind of integrity, deriving from the particular circumstances of their creation. Eventually, of course, they must all topple and die; but until that day comes, they can be allowed to make their way without substantial in course adjustments.

Besides, most of what is written here appears to me to have survived time's test. The parts that seemed newest and riskiest in 1970 have become as noted, progressively mainstreamed. Indeed, some of these parts have been bolstered by more recent work from different hands. The result, in broad terms, is a steady accretion of knowledge about early American family life. What this book aims to show for Plymouth people can now be compared to family patterns in other "Puritan" settlements, in Quaker communities of the Middle Colonies, among planters and yeomen of the early South, and in African-American and Native American groups of similar historical location. (See Bibliography, p. xiii.) There is no easy way to add up the score here. In some respects, the keynote is difference. (Family demography, for instance: Thus the favorable conditions of seventeenth-century Plymouth contrast sharply with what scholars have discovered for the early Chesapeake.) In others, there is a pervasive sameness (e.g., gender relations, with male preference being, virtually everywhere, the central theme). In all these areas, moreover, ample room remains for further work.

In the meantime, it is gratifying to think that *A Little Commonwealth* still has a contribution to make—and a role to play. I hope readers can experience some of the same pleasures of discovery that I had in writing the book many years ago.

Tyringham, Massachusetts   J. D.
November 1998

BIBLIOGRAPHY

to the Second Edition

✻

*What follows is a sampling of historical work on
early American family life published since the appearance of
A Little Commonwealth in 1970.*

Axtell, James, *The School Upon a Hill: Education and Society in Colonial New England* (1974).

Calvert, Karin, *Children in the House* (1992).

Fischer, David Hackett, *Growing Old in America* (1977).

Fox, Vivian C. and Martin H. Quitt, *Loving, Parenting, and Dying: The Family Cycle in England and America* (1980).

Frost, J. William, *The Quaker Family in Colonial America* (1973).

Greven, Philip J. Jr., *The Protestant Temperament: Patterns of Child-Rearing, Religious Experience, and the Self in Early America* (1977).

Jensen, Joan M., *Loosening the Bonds: Mid-Atlantic Farm Women, 1750-1850* (1986).

Koehler, Lyle, *A Searching for Power: The "Weaker Sex" in Seventeenth-Century New England* (1980).

Kulikoff, Allan, *Tobacco and Slaves: The Development of Southern Cultures in the Chesapeake* (1986).

Levy, Barry, *Quakers and the American Family: British Settlement in the Delaware Valley* (1982).

Lewis, Jan, *The Pursuit of Happiness: Family and Values in Jefferson's Virginia* (1983).

Norton, Mary Beth, *Founding Mothers and Fathers: Gendered Power and the Forming of American Society* (1996).

Slater, Peter Gregg, *Children in the New Eengland Mind: In Death and Life* (1977).

Smith, Daniel Blake, *Inside the Great House: Planter Family-Life in Eighteenth-Century Chesapeake Society* (1981).

Ulrich, Laurel Thatcher, *Good Wives: Image and Reality in the Lives of Women in Northern New England, 1650-1750* (1980).

Wall, Helena, *Fierce Communion: Family and Community in Early America* (1990).

FOREWORD

to the First Edition

The kind of study presented in this monograph has not as yet won a wide following among working historians. On the whole their interest has remained with the larger units of social action: the region, the class, the party, the ethnic or religious group. It has been left to the so-called behavioral sciences—anthropology, sociology, psychology—to demonstrate the fundamental importance of the smallest and most intimate of all group environments, the family.

Like most generalizations this one admits of certain important exceptions. Two outstanding books on the history of early American family life come to mind immediately, one published in 1944, the other in 1960.[1] Moreover, antiquarians and genealogists have long been concerned with particular aspects of particular families. And, during the past few years, there have been signs of a more concerted effort in the same overall direction from a new generation of historians, influenced in part by the work of certain

1. Edmund S. Morgan, *The Puritan Family* (New York, 1966); and Bernard Bailyn, *Education in the Forming of American Society* (Chapel Hill, N. C., 1960). Morgan's work was initially published as part of *More Books*, the Bulletin of the Boston Public Library, 1942–43. I should also acknowledge the classic, if now outdated, study by Arthur W. Calhoun, *A Social History of the American Family*, 3 vols. (Cleveland, 1917–18).

European colleagues, and in part by the ideas of the behavioral scientists.[2] Yet taken altogether, this work has not been enough to stake out a definite area of study, with its own boundaries, internal structure, and guiding themes and questions. There is as yet no sense of the major outlines of the story, and little agreement even about research procedures, source materials, and terminology.

In the face of so many uncertainties one response, more instinctive than reasoned, has been to descend to the level of local, almost personal history. It has seemed important to try to know average people in the everyday routine of their lives, in order to begin to understand their behavior in a family setting. Research of this kind bears at least a surface resemblance to the work of the antiquarians and in fact it draws quite heavily on materials that the latter have uncovered. But its purpose is different in an obvious and essential way; it aims ultimately for general answers, for a picture of *the* family rather than any single instance thereof.

My own work with Plymouth Colony is offered very much in the same spirit. This is, it seems, an unabashedly local study, for I have sought at every point to develop my analysis with materials indigenous to Plymouth. When, moreover, it has seemed helpful to refer to analogous circumstances in other colonies or regions, I have tried to do so quite explicitly—even apologetically. Yet at the same time I do hold to a larger purpose, and am somewhat concerned lest the title and subtitle of this book suggest merely one more exercise in antiquarianism. The danger is perhaps the greater when one has chosen to take as subjects the people of the "Old Colony" (as it has been known for many generations), the "Pilgrims" of fond and venerable legend. Let me therefore be quite candid about my belief that family life in Plymouth was not at all unique. There were, I think, broad lines of similarity to the typical case in the other American colonies, particularly those

---

2. I am thinking here of work such as that of Prof. Philip J. Greven, Jr., on the family in colonial Andover Mass., and Dr. Kenneth Lockridge on Dedham, Mass.

embraced by the term "Puritanism." The family is, after all, an extremely fundamental and durable institution: it often provides a kind of common denominator, or baseline, for a whole culture whose various parts may differ substantially in other respects. In short, I have wished to write a type of "case study" in early American family life—a study which, through sustained work on materials from one community, produces questions, methods of approach, and even some substantive conclusions that will ultimately have a much wider application.

Most investigations of family life in the fairly distant past are bedeviled by one fundamental circumstance: the subject is something which the people of the time took so much for granted that it seemed to require little formal comment. The situation for Plymouth does, however, present certain hopeful possibilities; and it may be well to indicate here, at the outset, the three types of source material on which I have relied most heavily. First, there are the physical artifacts that remain from the seventeenth century—houses (and house foundations), furniture, tools, utensils, clothing, and the like. Second, there is a large assortment of wills and inventories—documents which reveal much not only about the possessions of the colonists, but also about the inner relationships between different members of given families. And, third, there are the official records of the Colony (and also the records of individual towns). However, each kind of source carries with it certain inherent difficulties for the historian. The physical remains are quite literally dumb; one sees the object, but cannot automatically know all that its owner did with it or understand for certain the importance that he attached to it. The wills and inventories tend to reveal the most formal level of family interaction; it is only rarely that personal and emotional factors can be directly glimpsed. The Court records necessarily carry a kind of negative bias: they tell us what the community disapproved. Conspicuously missing from this checklist of sources are the literary materials—published books and essays, speeches, letters, journals, and other forms of personal comment and opinion— which often bulk largest in historical research. But this is precisely the kind of evidence which usually comes in short supply with regard to questions of family life—and particularly so in the case of Plymouth. There is only one such source that I have found consistently helpful in my own study; namely, the various essays collected in the *Works* of John Robinson, the original Pilgrim pastor.[3] There are also a few pertinent references in William Bradford's famous history,[4] but virtually nothing in the other written sources from the period.

Perhaps, however, this is not a wholly unfortunate circumstance for Edmund Morgan's excellent monograph, *The Puritan Family* (already cited above), can reasonably be appropriated to fill the void. Morgan has made good use of a fairly substantial body of literary materials from the early history of Massachusetts Bay—chiefly the sermons and essays of leading clergymen in that colony. It is safe to assume that the opinions expressed by such men would have found a ready assent at Plymouth as well; and they can, I think, stand in lieu of any statements by comparable figures in the Old Colony. Indeed, at the risk of seeming presumptuous, I venture to hope that my own work on Plymouth will be considered as broadly complementary to the Morgan book. Our findings, while not identical, make a good overall fit; yet our rather different angles of approach give each book a kind of independent base. Perhaps, in the end, there is one perceptible difference with respect to subject matter as well. For Morgan's extensive use of literary materials may tend to weight his conclusions toward the most affluent and educated class of people (particularly given a society that was only partially literate); whereas I, lacking such evidence for Plymouth, have tried

3. *The Works of John Robinson*, ed. Robert Ashton (Boston, 1853).
4. William Bradford, *Of Plymouth Plantation*, ed. Samuel Eliot Morison (New York, 1952).

quite self-consciously to reach the life of the "average man." But if this is so, it simply augments the complementary relationship between the two studies.

Every piece of historical research is an undertaking partly of description and partly of analysis, and I would like to use this opportunity to introduce certain methodological intentions which I have tried to apply to each side of my task. With regard to description, I have wished especially to limit the element of impressionistic presentation so common in historical writing— the tendency to offer a general statement followed (or preceded) by a small number of illustrative "examples." The drawbacks inherent in this method are obvious and constitute the chief argument for attempting to use "quantitative" measures whenever possible. Of course, in dealing with questions about the fairly distant past the historian usually finds only limited or fragmentary data; and, as I have been forced to recognize again and again in my work on Plymouth, there is often simply no alternative to the impressionistic approach. Still, in some particular matters I have contrived to present the situation in quantitative terms. Most such statements represent a "best possible guess" on the basis of materials that I have assembled about the lives of some 2000 Old Colony residents. Any *single* statement embraces only a part of the total sample, since for most individuals the information is not complete. Therefore none of this can be taken as definitive in the true meaning of the word. The chance to render precise statistical judgments, subject to careful verification, extends only to students of contemporary society (or perhaps of very recent history). But I do feel that such measures can be strongly suggestive, even for communities three hundred years in the past. In the particular case of the history of the family, they introduce a greater degree of precision into a field which heretofore has been widely influenced by popular myth, and indeed by the most careless sort of guesswork.

In the analytic side of their task historians usually profess, and practice, an essentially *ad hoc*, intuitive approach; and I have certainly presented my fair share of judgments of this type in the pages that follow. However, I have also tried at certain points to fit the evidence from Plymouth with appropriate *theoretical* models. Most of these are borrowed from the various branches of behavioral science in which the study of family life has been more extensively pursued. The historian's fundamental commitment to the study of individual facts, rather than the discovery of broad conceptual constructs, seems to me clear—and unexceptionable. But there is no reason why he cannot *use* theory to help with any given undertaking—in short, as a means to his own particular ends.

There are, to be sure, certain problems with this type of interdisciplinary borrowing, and one of the most immediate is the problem of language. The special terminologies of the relevant work in the behavioral sciences cannot easily be relocated in the midst of the usual historical narrative; and I have tried, whenever necessary, not only to transplant, but to trans*late* as well. I am not sure that I have always succeeded in this, but I do recognize the objections, both aesthetic and practical, to any really indiscriminate pattern of exchange.

And another sort of caution must also be entered here. I am a little fearful that the use of "theory" may seem to give an unduly speculative or hypothetical cast to certain parts of my discussion. But if so, I trust that they will be read in the spirit in which they were written—namely, as plausible, and useful, ways to make sense of materials that might otherwise be left to lie inert and unexplained. All of this reflects my own conviction that historians must be ready to consider interpretations, hypotheses, and even "hunches" that go some distance beyond the known facts. If, for example, a critic were to say to me that my argument in a later section does not finally establish the particular importance of "autonomy" in the development of Puritan children, I could only agree. But the demand for certainty—or at least for "proof"—while reasonable and laudable as a long-range goal, need not be rigidly maintained at every stage of historical inquiry. Proof is relative in any case—and scholars should never, in my opinion, dismiss an important problem because of "insufficient data." Particularly in the newer fields of research (like the history of the family), the framing of significant questions and of their probable answers may help to speed the recovery of the essential pieces of evidence. We must be ready to ponder what is *likely* to have happened—when more certain knowledge is lacking. We may then hope that future research in the same general area will turn up additional materials that serve either to strengthen such interpretations, or to modify them, or to put them down for good.

I want, finally, to say something about the overall plan of the book. An initial decision of considerable importance concerned the matter of organization; and, for two reasons, I chose to adopt a topical principle rather than a chronological one. All things considered, this seemed a better way to lend prominence to the analytic themes and issues, which in my own mind form a central part of the work. But, in addition, this choice can probably be justified by reference to the nature of the subject matter itself. I have already suggested that the family usually wears an aspect of similarity across a broad reach of geographical space within a single culture, and the same thing can be said of the time dimension as well. Change in the fundamental structure and character of family life always comes extremely slowly; in the language of anthropology, we are talking here of one of those "primary institutions" whose essential durability normally lends coherence to a wide range of more visible cultural processes.[5] It would therefore be hard to construct a meaningful account of this subject on the

5. The reference is, in particular, to the work of Abram Kardiner. For his usage of the terms "primary institution" and "secondary institution," see Abram Kardiner and Ralph Linton, *The Individual and His Society* (New York, 1939), 471–83.

basis of development through time, especially with terminal points that are less than a century apart. In some specific areas where change *was* discernible, and important, I have tried to call attention to the fact. But in the long run this is a story in which elements of stability and continuity loom unusually large.

Thus my book begins with a brief introductory essay which purports to offer a kind of overview of Plymouth Colony history. This, I hope, will be useful as "context" for the more focused and detailed discussion which follows; but readers already familiar with the story of the Old Colony may want to skip ahead to the main section of the text. Part One is an attempt to delineate the physical "stage" on which family life was acted out, to contrive a visual picture of the settlers as they went about their daily business. Part Two presents a discussion of the actual membership of Plymouth households, and the relationship in which individuals stood to one another within particular families. Part Three describes some of the major themes in the development of a typical settler from birth, through youth and adulthood, to old age and finally to death itself. And a concluding chapter evaluates, in a more general way, the fundamental sources of strength and of strain in these seventeenth-century families, with particular reference to their place in the community at large.

This whole project has been nourished from the start by the generosity of many friends, colleagues, and institutions. An important measure of financial assistance came originally from the Massachusetts Society of Mayflower Descendants, and was arranged through the good offices of Plimoth Plantation, Inc. The Plantation supplemented this grant out of its own funds, and has also provided many other forms of aid—clerical, editorial, administrative—as well as a simple but necessary kind of sympathetic encouragement. In this connection I would particularly like to thank Arthur Pyle and James Deetz, both of whom have followed the research from its inception and have examined the final product with discerning care. Among the others who have read and evaluated the manuscript, either in part or in whole, are Oscar Handlin, Philip Greven, Douglas Leach, Tamara Hareven, George Langdon, and Cary and Barbara Carson. Their thoughtful comments and criticisms have enabled me to improve my argument in a number of important particulars. Of course, in at least a few instances I have stubbornly clung to my original formulation; and for this and other reasons I hasten to discharge them of any larger responsibility for the book as it finally stands. I profited at an early stage from a long discussion of Plymouth Colony architecture with Richard Candee. Staff members at Pilgrim Hall and the Harlow House helped me to learn about the material artifacts of seventeenth-century life, and also allowed me to use photographs from both sites. Similar photographic permissions were granted by the committee in charge of the Major John Bradford House in Kingston. The pictures (at least some of them) were taken at my behest by Robert I. Frank. Rose T. Briggs of the Plymouth Antiquarian Society spent a whole afternoon initiating me into the mysteries of spinning, candle-making, and other domestic processes. Dr. Robert McGandy steered me to some important research in his own field (public health) bearing on questions of human fertility. Finally, Brandeis University provided funds for typing the manuscript and for the photography. To all these people and institutions I am indeed most grateful.

One last kind of indebtedness is extremely hard to specify, though it may well be the most important of all. All men have families of their own—even historians—and the personal ramifications of working on this particular subject are correspondingly complex. I have sensed at times that idiosyncratic concerns of my own might subtly intrude themselves in such a way as to distort my reading of the seventeenth-century family. This is what psychologists call "projection" and all scholars whose research touches the more intimate dimensions of human experience must watch carefully for its appearance. I cannot be sure that I have wholly suppressed it. At the same time I feel that any worthwhile insight this book may possess grows, in an absolutely essential way, from my experience with the members of my family. I had long anticipated the pleasure of writing the dedication to my parents; now, at almost the last moment, the pleasure has been suddenly crossed with grief. Words seem a most inadequate resource in the struggle to come to terms with death; but I want to express in this way my continuing affirmation of all the good and profound things that my father and I have been able to share. The contributions of my wife are many and diverse—and immeasurable. She was from the start an invaluable source of new ideas and perspectives, a patient tutor in all my efforts to forage in the thickets of the behavioral sciences, and a careful critic of my prose style. But most of all, she has always been there when it counted.

J.D.

Watertown, Mass.
September, 1969

CONTENTS

". . . a familie is a little Church, and a little commonwealth, at least a lively representation thereof, whereby triall may be made of such as are fit for any place of authoritie, or of subjection in Church or commonwealth. Or rather it is as a schoole wherein the first principles and grounds of government and subjection are learned: whereby men are fitted to greater matters in Church or commonwealth."

William Gouge
Of Domesticall Duties (London, 1622)

INTRODUCTION:
AN HISTORICAL SURVEY
OF PLYMOUTH COLONY

"Being thus arrived in a good harbor, and brought safe to land, they fell upon their knees and blessed the God of Heaven, who had brought them over the vast and furious ocean, and delivered them from all the perils and miseries thereof, again to set their feet on the firm and stable earth, their proper element." [1]

With these words William Bradford described the arrival of the Pilgrims in Provincetown harbor, their first landfall in the New World. Their story, in broad outline, has of course become a familiar one to many later generations of Americans. The *Mayflower*, the Compact, Plymouth Rock, Squanto, the romance of John and Priscilla Alden: all this belongs now to an important segment of what might be called our mythic national identity. Strangely, however, the formal scholarship of this subject has been quite limited. There was, for example, no full-length history of Plymouth Colony, conforming to accepted criteria of profes-

1. William Bradford, *Of Plymouth Plantation*, ed. Samuel Eliot Morison (New York, 1952), 61.

sional research, until very recently.[2] It is almost as if the aura of legend surrounding the Pilgrim settlers makes them difficult to recover as live human beings, caught up in a round of routine, everyday activities. Yet in most respects they were ordinary men of their time, and their experience was fundamentally similar to that of their neighbors in other colonies to the north and south. Indeed it might even be argued that this very quality—the whole thread of slow, steady, and unspectacular development—makes Plymouth an especially good "laboratory" for the study of early American life.

If any aspect of their history seemed to set off this particular group of settlers, it was their experience *before* reaching the New World. Their "pilgrimage" began with the formation of a distinctive type of religious community in England near the start of the seventeenth century, and led them to an initial period of voluntary exile in Holland. They belonged, of course, to the larger movement called Puritanism, and more particularly they were "separatists." [3] This meant that they declined any fellowship with the established church of the realm and sought instead to practice an austere form of "congregational" piety purged of the various corruptions that still (in their eyes) infested Anglicanism.

The nucleus of the original Pilgrim settlers was drawn from Scrooby, England, a small community about 150 miles to the north of London. They formed one of several separatist congregations in this area; and like the others, they were subjected to increasing levels of harassment by state authorities during the early years of the reign of King James I. By the summer of 1607 they had decided to remove themselves to Holland, where, in a climate

2. The gap has now been filled with the publication of George D. Langdon, Jr., *Pilgrim Colony: A History of New Plymouth, 1620–1691* (New Haven, Conn., 1966). This careful, admirably sound and sensible study should remain "definitive" for a long time to come. I have myself leaned heavily upon it at several points in this introductory chapter.
3. As demonstrated in Langdon, *Pilgrim Colony*, 100–107, the "separatism" of the Plymouth community lost meaning under the conditions of life in the New World.

of general toleration unusual for that era, they might be free to worship as they wished. After a brief stay in Amsterdam, they settled down to a sparse, but relatively tranquil, existence in the city of Leyden. There they remained for more than a decade. For the most part, it seems, they were allowed to go their own way; but they experienced a sense of strangeness and confinement that is perhaps unavoidable in any refugee community. They worried about their children growing up in an alien land. They chafed at their straitened economic circumstances, the need to work unceasingly in order to maintain a living standard that was little more than bare subsistence; and they wondered if they were growing old before their time. They observed with sorrow that few of their fellow communicants still in England cared to join them in this generally unpromising situation.[4] For such reasons they reached, in time, the decision to move once again. Now they would travel the whole breadth of the Atlantic Ocean—with the hope of re-establishing themselves in a land nominally English but effectively beyond the reach of regular state and ecclesiastical power.

But this was a large project, requiring a substantial measure of outside assistance. The colonists would need, in the first place, a "patent" from one of the chartered trading companies which the Crown had invested with official control over New World "plantations." They would need to recruit additional personnel. And above all they would need money—both to finance the actual voyage, and to maintain the settlement until it was able to become fully self-supporting. Negotiations began on several fronts in 1617, but were immediately beset with various forms of disappointment and delay. The financial problem was especially troublesome. The Pilgrims finally struck a bargain with a group of London merchants headed by an ironmonger named Thomas Weston, but on terms that seemed distressingly harsh. The entire output of the settlement was to remain common property for a period of seven

4. See Bradford, *Of Plymouth Plantation*, 23-25.

years, with the bulk of the "dividends" to go to the Weston group. Months of bitter haggling over these terms set a pattern that would continue, in the relations of the "planters" and the "adventurers," for many years thereafter.[5] Finally in 1620, unwilling to wait longer for a more favorable arrangement, an advance guard of 102 settlers embarked on the little *Mayflower* and set their course for the New World.

The settlers knew that the task of colonization would not be easy, but they could scarcely have imagined the extremity of the hardships that awaited them. They reached Plymouth a little before Christmas, just as winter was setting in. Weakened by the long period of confinement and inadequate nourishment on shipboard, they found soon enough that their very survival was in question. Sickness swept through the entire company, and within six months nearly half of them were dead. The arrival of spring seemed to bring a change in their luck. The tide of illness abated, and the survivors turned their thoughts toward planting. They were befriended by groups of Indians living nearby (including Squanto), and they derived from this source invaluable advice on local conditions for hunting, fishing, and agriculture. They would never again be quite so desperate as during that first winter, but for several years each new infusion of settlers placed heavy strains on their limited stores of provisions.

There were, too, worrisome kinds of *social* strain. Even while the *Mayflower* was still at sea "mutinous speeches" had been heard from a few of its passengers, and the famous Compact was a direct response to this threat of divisiveness. The signers of the Compact formally bound themselves together into a "Civil Body Politic" and agreed to be ruled by laws "most meet and convenient for the general good." But even so, almost from the first days ashore there were renewed "discontents and murmurings," which the leader-

5. For a full treatment of these and related problems, see Ruth A. McIntyre, *Debts Hopeful and Desperate: Financing the Plymouth Colony* (Plimoth Plantation, 1963).

ship could not finally dispel.[6] In fact, the Plymouth community was never as homogeneous as has usually been imagined. There were in the first group a number of "strangers"—people not primarily committed to religious aims and values—in contrast to the "pilgrims" themselves. In subsequent years there came others known as "particulars" because they had paid their own ("particular") way and could not therefore be asked to share in the debts of the Colony as a whole. Some individual "strangers" and "particulars" became trusted and valued citizens, but others continued to seem different and more or less suspect. They formed a kind of "out-group" and remained a reservoir of potential recruits for any insurgent movement that might arise within the Colony. Thus, for example, the storm of controversy aroused in 1625 by the Rev. John Lyford, the first clergyman to come to Plymouth, seems to have taken shape along the lines of cleavage between regular "planters" and "particulars." [7] This was a uniquely vivid case of conflict, but perhaps in other, smaller and more subterranean ways the same struggle was continually re-enacted through the early years of the Colony.

These early years were, necessarily, a time of some uncertainty and flux in the affairs of Plymouth. With social divisions present from the start, and with few clear precedents for the organization of an entirely new settlement, it could hardly have been otherwise. But by about 1640 the Colony had begun to achieve a measure of stability, at least in institutional terms. An underlying framework of Church and State, validated by the test of experience, was increasingly evident. There would, of course, be alterations in some parts of this framework during the years ahead, but its chief structural characteristics seemed established.

The ultimate unit of political participation and power was the

6. See Bradford, *Of Plymouth Plantation*, 75–77.
7. See Langdon, *Pilgrim Colony*, 21 ff.

individual "freeman." This was a formal status for which all adult male householders might directly apply. Approval was based on general considerations of character and competence; unlike the Massachusetts Bay Colony, Plymouth set no specific requirements in terms of church membership. Some applications did not succeed (for reasons that unfortunately went unrecorded), but recent research has suggested that a majority were accepted.[8] Initially the "freemen" themselves composed the General Court, which enacted all necessary "laws and ordinances," voted "rates" (taxes), and (after 1640) supervised the distribution of lands. In 1638 the Colony switched to a system of representation, whereby the householders of each town elected "deputies" to serve on the Court. Within the Court a place of special eminence was accorded the "magistrates"—the Governor and his seven Assistants. These men, chosen annually, formed the highest judicial body in the Colony, and (especially during the early years) exercised considerable day-to-day administrative authority as well. Over time the powers officially vested in the Assistants would contract somewhat, but they retained great influence of an informal kind. Sometimes their policies were rejected by the rest of the General Court, occasionally they themselves were voted out of office; by and large, however, they provided an enduring and respected form of leadership for the community as a whole. Clearly in most matters of wider significance their opinions were decisive. Within this group the Governor was a strong first among equals. No man in the history of Plymouth Colony wielded such influence as William Bradford (who was Governor during most of the years between 1621 and 1656); but later governors, like Thomas Prence, were also powerful figures.

More important to the average person than these Colony-wide institutions were the various systems of town government. The

8. See George D. Langdon, Jr., "The Franchise and Political Democracy in Plymouth Colony," *William and Mary Quarterly*, 3d Ser., XX (1963), 513–26.

fundamental agency here was the "meeting" of all resident householders, convened at regular intervals to debate and vote "orders"
relevant to common needs and purposes. Most towns elected a
group of "selectmen" to manage their affairs during the periods
between meetings. A variety of lesser offices were also created
(largely on English models)—fence-viewers, surveyors of high-
ways, raters, constables, a treasurer; and *ad hoc* committees were
frequently appointed to attend to some special question. These institutions arose more or less spontaneously, since there was no explicit provision for them in the early laws of the Colony. Indeed
the General Court often seemed reluctant to recognize them; the
right of towns to choose selectmen, for instance, was not formally
authorized until 1665.

Equally central to the life of local communities was, of course,
the church. Each town was also a "congregation" (or, in later
years, two or three congregations), and its corporate sense of itself depended largely on common traditions of religious belief and
worship. The churches of Plymouth, like Puritan churches elsewhere, maintained a fundamental distinction between those who
had been "converted" and "owned the covenant," and those who
had not. Only the former were eligible for church membership.
Yet these standards were applied rather liberally—more so, perhaps, than in some of the churches of Massachusetts Bay. Individual candidates were asked to make some profession as to their
inner experience of God's grace, but they were not required to
submit to any detailed cross-examination. Thus in practice a considerable part of the adult population would sooner or later become church members.

Each of the churches in the Old Colony managed its own affairs
and resisted on principle any idea of a larger system of ecclesiastical control. Each church hired its own minister, determined the
order of its service, and conducted a variety of administrative
business. It also sat in judgment on the errant deeds of its own
membership. Its records were dotted with motions of censure and

(less often) with formal proceedings of excommunication. The range of offenses was considerable: fornication, swearing, drunkenness, "insolency," and other types of "scandalous carriage." While censure and excommunication carried no legal force outside the congregation and did not necessarily lead to civil or criminal prosecution, they were still effective sanctions. At the very least they must have imposed a degree of social ostracism on the individuals directly involved.

To sketch, as we have just now been doing, the various institutional systems of Plymouth Colony is to emphasize those aspects of life which most clearly expressed the whole theme of control. The General Court considering the admission of new freemen, the Court of Assistants punishing a man for slander, the town ordering the repair of broken fences, the church voting to censure a wayward communicant—here are images enough of authority, of discipline, even of repression. All this was real and important in the day-by-day experience of the settlers, but it was only *one side* of that experience. Unfortunately, too, it is the side to which an earlier era of scholarship gave an excessive, almost exclusive, kind of attention. But if we look carefully, if, in particular, we try to keep individual lives clearly in focus, we gradually uncover a rather different set of themes and tendencies. We uncover an area of life that was profoundly characterized by elements of movement and change—indeed by a kind of fluidity that is commonly associated with a much later period in our national history.

No aspect of this situation seems more striking in retrospect than the simple factor of geographical mobility. Some of the original Plymouth settlers began to take up lots across the river in Duxbury even before 1630; among them were such prominent figures as John Alden, Myles Standish, and Jonathan Brewster. The process was accelerated by the establishment to the north of the Massachusetts Bay Colony. An important new market for cattle and corn was thereby opened up, and the compact town of Plymouth was not large enough to meet the demand for increased

production. In 1636 the town of Scituate was officially incorporated, and by the end of the next decade eight more new towns
had been established. The direction of the earliest expansion was
north and south along the coast; then a westerly thrust began,
which led to the founding of such towns as Taunton, Rehoboth,
Bridgewater, and Middleborough, all well inland. Still other
groups of people pushed onto Cape Cod; indeed in the early
1640s there was a move to abandon the original settlement at
Plymouth altogether and relocate the town on the outer cape.
This proposal was finally defeated after much discussion in the
meetings of the freemen, but some families went anyway, on their
own, and founded the town of Eastham.

These events greatly distressed some of the leaders of the Colony, who believed that the achievement of their goals, the whole
effort to establish a truly Godly community, would depend on
maintaining a close and compact pattern of settlement. Periodically they sought to stem the tide. Thus on several occasions when
new land was parceled out, the General Court directed that it be
used only for actual settlement by the grantees themselves.[9] Also
the Court criticized the unrestrained way in which lands were distributed by the freemen in certain of the newer townships. Grants
were no longer confined to upright, religious-minded settlers;
towns accepted, with no questions asked, almost anyone who proposed to move in.[10] William Bradford was one of the people to
whom all of this came as a keen disappointment; it runs through
his famous history of Plymouth as a kind of tragic refrain. "This I
fear will be the ruin of New England, at least of the churches of

9. See *Records of the Colony of New Plymouth, in New England,* ed.
Nathaniel B. Shurtleff and David Pulsifer (Boston, 1855–61), II, 9. Also
Bradford, *Of Plymouth Plantation,* 253–54.
10. Such was the charge leveled against the people of Sandwich, for
example, in 1639. A similar situation seems to have prevailed in Yarmouth,
for in 1640 the Court specifically directed the town elders there to require
of each new arrival a "certificate from the places whence they come . . .
of their religious and honest carriage." See *Plymouth Colony Records,* I,
131, 142.

God there," he wrote at one point, "and will provoke the Lord's displeasure against them." [11] When the plan for moving the town to Eastham was debated, Bradford, and others of like mind, discerned the real motive behind the proposal: "Some were still for staying together in this place, alleging men might here live if they would be content with their condition, and that it was not for want or necessity so much that they removed as for the enriching of themselves." [12]

Yet the process of dispersion, begun so very early, was never halted. The magnetic influence of empty land was too powerful, and people of every age and condition yielded to it. They moved, sometimes as individuals and sometimes in groups, edging further and further away from the original center at Plymouth. New towns arose in the wilderness and were chartered, albeit reluctantly, by the General Court.[13] There were also numerous smaller villages and hamlets, that went officially unrecognized but grew and prospered nonetheless. The physical aspect of the Old Colony after mid-century seems to have been rather arbitrary and disorganized, with a straggling chain of settlements of varying shapes and sizes, and even some isolated homesteads, flung out over a very broad expanse of territory.[14]

The dispersion of settlement was part of a larger change whereby the community left behind the ideals of the first set-

11. Bradford, *Of Plymouth Plantation*, 254.
12. Bradford, *Of Plymouth Plantation*, 333.
13. The towns of Plymouth Colony, in the order of their incorporation, were as follows: Plymouth, 1620; Scituate, 1636; Duxbury, 1637; Barnstable, 1639; Taunton, 1639; Sandwich, 1639; Yarmouth, 1639; Marshfield, 1641; Rehoboth, 1645; Eastham, 1646; Bridgewater, 1656; Dartmouth, 1664; Swansea, 1667; Middleborough, 1669; Edgartown, 1671; Tisbury, 1671; Little Compton, 1682; Freetown, 1683; Rochester, 1686; Falmouth, 1686; Nantucket, 1687.
14. I have tried elsewhere to describe these expansive pressures in more detail. See John Demos, "Notes on Life in Plymouth Colony," *William and Mary Quarterly*, 3d Ser., XXII (1965), 264-86.

tlers—a change which another student of the period has aptly described as leading "from Puritan to Yankee." [15] The motion was spiritual as well as spatial: this, of course, is what men like Bradford sensed in pleading so strenuously against it. Yet the overall trend was a very gradual one, and its effects became clear only with the passage of several generations. Indeed the danger for us, from our vantage point of three centuries later, is that we may fail to appreciate the forces of tradition, the old ways and values—and especially the power of religion. No part of our imaginative effort at historical reconstruction is more difficult. For like the life of the family, the life of religion—especially its interior dimensions, its reverberations in the thoughts and feelings and behavior of the average believer—was not systematically recorded.[16]

We should not therefore be surprised if, in the investigations that follow, religion seems to figure in a somewhat haphazard and occasional way. It was simply too basic, too much an assumed constant of life to be rendered fully visible and self-conscious. It registered largely as a kind of underlying presence, part of the very atmosphere which surrounded and suffused all aspects of experience. There were, however, clear symbols of its importance: the Bible treasured in nearly every home (including many where no

15. Richard L. Bushman, *From Puritan to Yankee* (Cambridge, Mass., 1967). This study deals chiefly with Connecticut in the eighteenth century. It is my contention (not Bushman's) that the same overall model of change can be applied to the older Puritan colonies two and three generations earlier. Perhaps, indeed, the whole concern with "declension"—with loss of original purpose—should not be linked too closely with changes through time in the *reality* of Puritan life. For it may also reflect an underlying conflict in the Puritan *psyche,* a conflict that was present virtually from the earliest phase of New England history.
16. This rather sweeping statement may, I realize, lend itself to some misunderstanding. Owing to the work of Perry Miller and a whole corps of his distinguished students, the religious faith and belief of the Puritan *leaders* is very well known indeed. But I am thinking rather of the *followers,* the ordinary citizens of these early New England towns. What they heard and read did not necessarily coincide with what their ministers and magistrates said and wrote. Thus I contend that we have an excellent picture of Puritan worship for the highest level of the culture (the educated, the powerful), but nothing comparable for the "average man." The problem in studying the latter group, of course, is that most of them were from the standpoint of history quite inarticulate.

other book was found); the meetinghouse strategically placed so as to dominate the entire village; the rhythm of life totally broken on Sundays for long hours of worship and meditation. Religion framed the essential standards of conduct, and served to "explain" every manner of event, large and small, happy and painful, public and private. Church and State were formally separate, but in practice they were everywhere intertwined.[17] Church attendance (for everyone, including non-members) was required by law; "heretical" views were suppressed; and periodically the Court might declare "solemn days of humiliation by fasting, etc., and also for thanksgiving as occasion shall be offered." [18]

Another long leap of imagination is required of us when we try to reconstruct the relationship of the settlers to their physical surroundings. They were, in the first place, virtually all farmers: even the tradesman, the artisan, and the minister would spend some regular portion of time working the land.[19] Thus their lives were geared to the basic rhythms of Nature in a way that may be hard for modern "metro-Americans" to understand. Weather conditions, for example, were of overwhelming significance: it is no accident that most personal diaries from this period are about 50 per cent meteorology. The pattern of the seasons created a powerful cycle of change to which many other aspects of experience, material and emotional, were irrevocably bound. In wintertime the dimensions of life profoundly—and quite literally—contracted, the day was shortened by several hours, and simple considerations of physical comfort became a constant and pressing concern. As spring came, life moved outdoors and the urgent business of planting gave point to a broad range of individual and community energies. Through the summer the crops grew, while men watched, and pruned, and weeded, and (in late July and August) turned to the heavy work of haying. The fall brought harvest time, the cli-

17. See Langdon, *Pilgrim Colony*, ch. 5, for a full discussion of these matters.
18. *Plymouth Colony Records*, XI, 18.
19. A most useful account of agriculture in the Old Colony is Darrett B. Rutman, *Husbandmen of Plymouth* (Boston, 1967).

mactic event in the whole sequence. Here was a kind of focus for hope and anxiety: in a few short weeks of intense activity, the rewards of a whole year's labor were concentrated. This, of course, was the immediate context of the first Thanksgiving—which, in turn, became the prototype of all similar occasions in later years.

Thus for the settlers Nature was an annual clock with which their lives turned in lock-step precision. Thus, too, it was the direct source of the tangible bounty on which their survival depended. But this was only half of the total picture, for in other ways and at other times it loomed as an adversary, a barrier, and a fearsome threat to peace and security. Surely no part of the American environment was more striking than the vast stretch of forest, extending virtually to the outer edge of the ocean shore. Massive, dark, dense, it must be attacked at once if men were to succeed in gaining any substantial foothold here. There was, moreover, little in the prior experience of the first settlers to prepare them for this aspect of their New World encounter, since much of England had long since been reduced to cultivation and heavily wooded lands were confined to the far north and west. The situation was compounded, of course, by the presence *within* the forest of Indians. Most of the people of Plymouth had no familiarity at all with a radically different culture. True, some of them had lived for a time in Holland, but at least the Dutch were of the same color and physical type, they worshiped the same God, they shared with Englishmen certain elements of a broad historical tradition. Plainly the strangeness of the American Indians was of another order altogether.

Still, the record of the Old Colony in its relations with the Indians was for many years quite impressive. The major tribe in the area was the Wampanoag, based on the "Mount Hope peninsula" and ruled when the Pilgrims arrived by a wise and benevolent chieftain named Massasoit. Both sides, settlers and Indians, wished from the outset to establish a pattern of stable and friendly contacts. Their leaders extended official hospitality to one another, exchanged gifts, and—more important—initiated a set of working procedures for trade and the transfer of lands.[20] The Colony exercised careful supervision over the actions of its own citizens: for example, individual settlers were forbidden to purchase land from Indians without formal authorization by the General Court.[21] For forty years the two peoples lived alongside one another in a state of peace, and even of amity. Inevitably personal conflicts flared from time to time, but they were effectively contained and resolved on their own terms; they did not lead on to larger difficulties.

This whole fortunate situation depended partly on the personal influence of the leaders of each group, and partly on considerations of geography. As long as Bradford and Massasoit were shaping policy, and as long as there was ample space for both communities, friendship continued. But after 1660 there was change on both counts. The growing population of the Colony created powerful pressures for further expansion; and the General Court responded by allowing some new settlement nearer than ever before to the Wampanoag lands at Mt. Hope. This meant increased contact between the two peoples, and a higher level of quarrels over such things as title boundaries and errant livestock. Meanwhile Bradford had died in 1657, Massasoit in 1660, and the new leaders on both sides, while surely not eager for conflict, were less deeply committed to the ways of peace. The pattern of developments in the years that followed was variable and complex, but the overall trend of Indian-settler relations was unmistakably downhill. The end result was the single most traumatic event in the whole history of the Old Colony, the waging of King Philip's War.[22]

Philip was a younger son of Massasoit who had come to the chieftainship of the Wampanoags in 1662; and it was he who

20. See Bradford's account of the earliest contacts with Indians. *Of Plymouth Plantation*, 79–84.
21. The law to this effect was passed in 1643. See *Plymouth Colony Records*, XI, 41.
22. The standard account of King Philip's War is Douglas Leach, *Flintlock and Tomahawk* (New York, 1958). See also Langdon, *Pilgrim Colony*, chs. 12, 13.

opened direct hostilities with an attack on the town of Swansea in June, 1675. For the next fifteen months all energy on both sides was turned to fighting. The pace of events was irregular, slowing considerably in wintertime, but the substance was uniformly tragic and terrifying. Other areas of New England were quickly drawn in—other colonies, other Indian tribes. It was essentially a guerrilla war, of a type that might well seem painfully familiar to Americans in the 1960s. The Indians made effective use of their greater knowledge of the forest, probing relentlessly for weak spots in the Colony's defenses, striking hard and without warning, and retreating just as fast. The settlers, for their part, were torn between conflicting needs and pressures. On the one hand they must defend their separate towns and villages; on the other, they must go after the enemy in force and destroy his power once and for all. In time their greater resources in terms of arms and food supplies turned the struggle in their favor, and by the fall of 1676 the Indians were wholly defeated. Philip himself was caught and killed (his body was quartered and left to rot); and many of his warriors and their families were sold into slavery in the West Indies. However, the losses sustained by the Colony had also been enormous—including a *per capita* rate of mortality higher than in any subsequent American war.[23] Indians would never again trouble this part of New England, but memories of havoc and horror would long remain.

Having survived this convulsive conflict with their Indian neighbors, the colonists were soon experiencing another sort of encroachment. In 1686 the British Crown began a sweeping reorganization of its imperial possessions, which (among other things) joined Plymouth with Rhode Island, Connecticut, and Massachusetts Bay in a single "Dominion of New England." On the whole Plymouth played a secondary role in this particular drama. The chief concern of the Crown was Massachusetts, where disregard

23. Langdon argues that between 5 and 8 per cent of the adult men in the Colony were lost during the War. See *Pilgrim Colony*, 181–82.

for royal authority was a long-established tradition. Plymouth, by contrast, had maintained a posture of obedient subordination and had acquired a relatively good reputation in the mother country. Her one failing was the lack of a valid charter,[24] and in the 1680s there was reason to hope that even this would be remedied. But the establishment of the Dominion ended all such hopes: the claims of Plymouth were easily brushed aside in the drive to impose a tighter, more centralized form of imperial control.

During the next three years the people of Plymouth suffered Dominion government very much as their fellow colonists to the north and west. They resented paying taxes to a government in which they were not effectively represented; they worried about the security of their titles to land; they resisted the disestablishment of their (Congregational) churches. The Dominion also created some special difficulties for the Old Colony—such as the many sorts of inconvenience involved in the transfer of the seat of government to Boston. Most men adjusted as best they could but hoped for another, more favorable turn of affairs. In fact, of course, the Dominion was very short-lived. It disintegrated completely in the spring of 1689, a direct casualty of the Glorious Revolution in England.

When the news reached Plymouth, the old leaders sought at once to re-establish the Colony government. Thomas Hinckley, the Governor just before the Dominion period, convened a meeting of representatives from all the towns; and these men, in turn, arranged for the election of a regular General Court. Moreover the leaders initiated new measures to secure a permanent charter for the Colony. Yet the old forms of government were never fully restored. The effort continued for two years, but they were years of frustration and disappointment for Governor Hinckley and his associates. Many settlers seemed ill-disposed towards their author-

24. Technically Plymouth Colony passed through her entire history with no more substantial right to exist than a land "patent" obtained from the old Council of New England in 1629. This did not confer the right of self-government—hence the desire to obtain a royal "charter."

ity, and a mood of restlessness was widely manifest. Matters reached a crisis when the Court voted new taxes in order to support Massachusetts Bay in a campaign against the French (who were just then ranging down from Canada). Several Old Colony towns simply refused to pay their share.

In the meantime, overseas, the status of all the New England colonies was under consideration by the advisers to the new king. Plymouth's request for a charter was only one aspect of a whole, complex sequence of negotiations. The Crown apparently felt that the Old Colony would be better served (particularly in terms of defense) by being joined to one of her larger neighbors. Perhaps she might have saved her independence by pressing vigorous appeals at Whitehall, but in fact she did not choose to do so. With the various towns divided, and with civil authority generally at a discount, there was neither the means nor the will for such an undertaking. In October 1691 the Crown issued a new charter for Massachusetts Bay, which also ordered the annexation of Plymouth.

Few men mourned the passing of the Old Colony. Scattered gestures of protest against the annexation died away within a year or two. In fact, Plymouth had long since lost her distinctive identity; in both economic and moral terms she was increasingly a direct dependent of Massachusetts Bay. Gone as a historical reality, she lived on for later generations of Americans—in legend.

PART ONE

THE PHYSICAL SETTING

Perhaps the safest way to make a first approach to the subject of family life in the Old Colony is to explore the actual physical remains from the period. Objects that one can see and touch and hold—and even use—give to the modern-day investigator a natural sense of security. Here, one feels, there are no mysteries; here there are none of those half-descriptions, hidden assumptions, or symbolic meanings which our own time does not and cannot fathom. Here the process of recovery is straightforward and sure.

Or is it? Unfortunately the matter is much more complex than it first seems. Go to Plymouth today, visit one of the old houses still so lovingly preserved, sit in one of the high-backed chairs, and try to "live" for a bit in the middle of the seventeenth century. It is a chastening experience. The objects are all right there before you, solid, tangible, real; but gradually they begin to dance before your eyes. Some of them, you feel, *must* have been placed here or there and used in this or that way; functional considerations seem obvious and decisive. But for others the picture is much less clear.

Alternative possibilities begin to suggest themselves: chairs move, dinnerware disappears, pots change places, lamps and heddles and buckets hang uncertainly in midair. There seem to be a thousand ways in which these things could be arranged, this amount of space used—and indeed there *are* a thousand ways.

The longer one "lives" with such physical objects, the more elusive they become. For the truth is that they are ultimately just what people make of them. Insofar as they cannot be connected with the specific individuals to whom they belonged, they are inert and possess no significance beyond pure antiquarianism. But our own efforts to make these connections must perforce be largely inferential, and often the inference we choose is only the best of several. Each object, moreover, must be considered in a variety of different ways. The questions of use and spatial positioning may seem easy enough in a given case, but in answering them we do not exhaust the subject. More difficult questions remain, questions that go right to the heart of any really profound understanding of family life. How did people *feel* about this or that object? What kind of value did they place upon it? What associations, voluntary or involuntary, did it call up in them? How might it influence, or reflect, the pattern of relationships that obtained between different members of the household? These are matters that we take for granted with respect to the familiar "objects" of our own lives; they belong to an area of unspoken, and sometimes unconscious, assumptions, habits, and beliefs. They represent a kind of underlying *context*, from which each particular object derives much of its true meaning. It is, however, just this kind of context which so often eludes us, in the study of the seventeenth or of any other century. Take, by way of concrete example, one rather common household item, the sieve. Its everyday function seems transparently clear; presumably there has been little change in this regard from 1650 to our own day. But turn now to the area of mental and emotional connections and consider that in the seventeenth century sieves were also used by conjurers and

magicians in obscure ceremonies of fortune-telling.[1] These were
matters full of danger but also of fascination, the kind of thing to
be discussed only in low tones and with trusted friends and neighbors. Is, then, a twentieth-century sieve equivalent to a seventeenth-century one? Or think, too, for a moment about the matter
of books. We know that in many Plymouth households books
might be found—but it is not always clear that the owners could
read them.[2] How and why were they valued? Did their possession
impart prestige? Did they serve as mementos of a more genteel
past or as symbols of the hope for a more ample future? Were

1. For a fuller discussion of these occult associations with sieves, see
George Lyman Kittredge, *Witchcraft in Old and New England* (Cambridge, Mass., 1929), 198 ff.
2. The inventory of a given man's estate usually contained a careful listing
of all his books, and in some cases we find that the same man had signed
his will with only a "mark." See, for example, the will and inventory of
Thomas Lapham of Scituate, *Mayflower Descendant*, X, 198–200; of William Thomas of Marshfield, X, 162–64; and of Thomas Hicks of Scituate,
XI, 160–61. Yet it must be confessed that there are some great uncertainties
connected with the analysis of this matter. Undoubtedly there were certain
men who could read but not write. And there is also evidence that sometimes even a fully literate man would sign a legal document with a "mark"
—a practice that harked back to the still older use of a personal seal rather
than a signature. My line of argument assumes, further, that if the husband
was illiterate, the other members of his family were likely to be so as
well. Certainly far fewer women (wives) than men could write in that
era; and there is little reason to think that the younger generation was
better off in this respect than its elders. (Indeed in some areas there may
have been an actual decline in overall literacy during the first decades after
settlement, since schooling under New World conditions was a most irregular process.) My chief authority here is Dr. Kenneth Lockridge—for
whose help in these matters I would like to acknowledge a special debt of
gratitude. Dr. Lockridge is currently finishing a monograph on the issue
of signature-mark literacy in colonial New England which will challenge
the earlier data on seventeenth-century Massachusetts cited in Samuel
Eliot Morison, *The Puritan Pronaos* (New York, 1936), ch. 3. Morison
seemed to accept from these data the *fact* that 90 per cent of the population could sign their names (and probably also read), but Lockridge argues
that this figure is distorted by the use of heavily biased source materials.
He has employed other sources, themselves still biased toward literacy but
less so than those of his predecessors, to arrive at a "substantially lower"
figure. He concludes that a "large minority" of the male population was not
literate in any sense, and that the "overwhelming majority" of women
shared the same limitation. (K. Lockridge, personal communication.)

they simply a good financial investment? What, indeed, is the significance of books in any half-literate community? Surely the situation must stand in considerable contrast to what we know from our own experience.

In the narrative that follows little enough will appear to throw light on such questions. But it is well perhaps to recognize at the outset the existence of this murky, largely unexplored, vitally important territory.[3] Antiquarians have scarcely approached it, absorbed as they are with the appreciation of artifacts *qua* artifacts. Historians, on the other hand, have felt more comfortable with the study of literary sources than with hard physical remains. Perhaps in the future these two groups will find ways to collaborate more often, with results that will measurably deepen our knowledge of social history. For the present we must try at least to find the essential questions to ask of our materials, even though the answers are not readily forthcoming.

3. For a more elaborate statement of some of the same ideas, see Lewis R. Binford, "Archaeology as Anthropology," in *American Antiquity*, XXVIII (1962), 217-25. Binford, indeed, points the way to a broad new view of the handling of physical evidence, which antiquarians—and historians—would do well to ponder.

CHAPTER ONE

HOUSING

❧

It is, of course, difficult to imagine any community with completely uniform housing, and no account of Plymouth would be accurate which did not attempt to reflect the range and variety of buildings to be found there.[1] The history of domestic architecture

1. In writing this whole section on "The Physical Setting" of Old Colony life I have been forced to lean heavily on the research of a variety of specialists in such matters. With regard to housing I must mention, in particular, some extremely useful work carried out in recent years under the overall sponsorship of Plimoth Plantation, Inc. Much of this work has been summarized in a document entitled "1966 Report on Architecture at Plimoth Plantation" (unpublished) by two of the principal investigators, Cary Carson and Richard M. Candee. See also certain emendations of this report, in the notes of the "Conference on Architecture of the Pilgrim Houses" (Sept. 25, 1967). Copies of both these documents are on file at Plimoth Plantation. The work of Carson and Candee has supplemented, and in some particulars revised, the earlier research of Charles Strickland. (See his "The Architecture of Plimoth Plantation," also unpublished.) I have also profited from conversations with James Deetz, now Assistant Director of the Plantation, who has been conducting some important excavations of Old Colony foundation sites. Nearly all of the work cited in this footnote has been directed to ends more truly (and literally) "architectural" than my own; that is, it aims to guide the Plantation in constructing with as much accuracy as possible a facsimile "Pilgrim Village." Thus, in shifting the focus somewhat—to the matter of the relationship between architecture and all

in Plymouth is a history of steadily growing diversity, so that by the end of the century the distance between the most humble and the most capacious houses of the colony was quite substantial. Especially striking was the readiness of the settlers to improvise, to add something here and change something there. Nonetheless three major "types" may be distinguished with respect to floor plan and means of construction; and these, when joined to certain fairly common variants, provide a convenient way of organizing a discussion.

The first type of housing in point of time can be dealt with fairly quickly, for its importance in the colony as a whole did not outlast the very earliest years.[2] It was in its essentials a small, crude, one-story building, without a real frame and built chiefly of wattle and daub. It was what the English called a "cottage"; to us it would probably have seemed the meanest kind of "hut." It was normally just one room, though in some cases there may have been a tiny loft just under the roof. Its chimney was made from logs covered with clay. It possessed few, if any, windows. No examples of this type of structure survive today, so we cannot reasonably try to describe it in detail. But it was, in any case, regarded by its builders as only a temporary form of shelter. The *May-flower* passengers knew that they would need months or years to prepare the construction of more substantial houses—and in the meantime they had to have some place to live.

---

the intangibles of family life—I am presenting conclusions for which my authorities can in no way be held responsible.

2. The documentary evidence for this type of housing is extremely thin. William Bradford mentions, in retrospect, the "small cottages" of the earliest years; see *Of Plymouth Plantation*, ed. Samuel Eliot Morison (New York, 1952), 76. There are several references to the gathering of thatch for roofing among the early entries in *A Journal of the Pilgrims at Plymouth: Mourt's Relation*, ed. Dwight B. Heath (New York, 1963), 43–45; and the same writer notes a bad storm in February, 1621 which "caused much daubing of our houses to fall down." *Ibid.*, 48. For a more detailed treatment of this subject see Carson and Candee, "Report on Architecture," "Appendix I: Plymouth's Earliest Architecture, 1620–25," by Richard M. Candee.

It would be interesting to know what became of these first Plymouth structures later on. Quite likely some were converted into barns, sheds, or other outhousing, and maintained for many years longer. Storage space was always at a premium in these households, and of course domestic animals required some type of shelter. There is no evidence, incidentally, that such animals were kept in some part of the main house—as is true in certain "peasant cultures" of our own day. All in all, therefore, it is hard to imagine the destruction of any form of housing, no matter how primitive. It is also just possible that the poorest class of settlers continued to live in this same type of dwelling for some time after the rest of the community had abandoned it. One wonders, for example, about a listing in the inventory of the estate of a certain Web Adey, an extremely poor man who died in Plymouth in 1652. The listing reads: "one smale house and garden . . . £1 10s." [3] The valuation is extremely meager even by the standards of the time, and the use of the adjective "small" is unusual. Perhaps, indeed, the reference was just to size and nothing more; but possibly, too, Web Adey's house was different in *form* as well—was, in fact, a throwback to the time when the Pilgrims had only just come ashore.

In 1623 Emmanuel Altham described Plymouth as having "about twenty houses, four or five of which are very fair and pleasant"; [4] and five years later another visitor stated, "The houses are constructed of clapboards, with gardens also enclosed behind and at the sides with clapboards, so that their houses and courtyards are arranged in very good order." [5] These descriptions seem to imply a transition to the second and far more important phase

3. *Mayflower Descendant*, XI, 8.
4. See *Three Visitors to Early Plymouth*, ed. Sidney V. James (Plimoth Plantation, Inc., 1963), 24. This volume contains all of the extant letters of Altham that describe his visit to Plymouth, and a number of comparable ones by John Pory and Isaack de Rasieres.
5. This comment is by Isaack de Rasieres. *Ibid.*, 76.

of Plymouth architecture. Presumably the "very fair and pleasant" houses of which Altham speaks were solid frame-type structures, and probably they were covered with the clapboards which were soon in common use throughout the colony. Yet even this kind of housing was quite modest by the standards then prevailing in England. William Bradford writes of one group of settlers who came to Plymouth in 1623 that they "looked for greater matters than they found or could attain unto, about building great houses and such pleasant situations for them as themselves had fancied; as if they would be great men and rich all of a sudden. But they proved castles in the air." [6]

Leaving aside, then, the castles in the air, what shall we say of the much less grand but more tangible structures that the settlers actually raised on the hard ground of Plymouth? It is surprising, first of all, that they were not larger. Many of the houses in the Old Colony were initially built to simple story-and-a-half, single-bay specifications. This is difficult to understand in view of the fact that in the mother country similar housing was rapidly disappearing. It survived only among the lowest segments of English society, laborers and poor farmers—people, in short, at least one rung lower on the social ladder than the groups from which the colonists themselves were chiefly recruited. Thus, according to the most careful recent students of Plymouth architecture, many settlers ought to have looked on their homes as "decidedly substandard housing." [7] Yet so far as we know they did not especially complain. The question of why there were so many houses built according to this single-bay plan cannot be answered with any confidence. It is easy enough to point to the sluggish economy of the region, yet most of the settlers achieved as individuals a fairly respectable standard of living.

The frames of these houses were put together from heavy oak

6. Bradford, *Of Plymouth Plantation,* 133.
7. Carson and Candee, "Report on Architecture," 5.

timbers, and the walls were either of clapboards or broad planks placed vertically between the end posts. (The latter alternative, incidentally, seems to have been a local style; [8] only a few similar examples have been found elsewhere in New England.) Thatch served for roofing on most of the houses built before 1635. After this time, however, there was a strong shift toward the use of boards and shingles; for thatch was a fire hazard. The earliest accounts of the colony by Bradford and Mourt,[9] contain numerous references to damaging fires; and the records of the court show repeated efforts by men in authority to find ways of minimizing the danger.[10] As for windows, they were normally few in number, and quite small in size.[11] The colonists seem to have wanted it this way, probably because of the difficulty in heating such houses in the wintertime. Until about 1640 most windows were made from

8. This kind of siding can be observed on three of the seventeenth-century houses that are still standing at Plymouth—the Churchill house, the Howland house, and the Sparrow house.

9. See *Of Plymouth Plantation*, 136, for an account of a fire which "broke out of the chimney into the thatch and burned down three or four houses and consumed all the goods and provisions in them." This wording may indicate a daub chimney (see below, p. 30) as well as a roof of thatch. See also Heath, *Journal of the Pilgrims*, 47, 48.

10. In 1627, for example, "It was agreed Upon by the whole Court . . . that from hence forward no dwelling house was to be covered with any kind of thatche, as straw, reeds, etc., but with either bord or pale & the like; to wit; of all that were to be new built in the towne." *Records of the Colony of New Plymouth, in New England*, ed. Nathaniel B. Shurtleff and David Pulsifer (Boston, 1855–61), XI, 4. Ten years later, however, the Court seemingly recognized that such legislation had not been altogether effective, for it ordered that every house have "one sufficient ladder" to reach the top of the roof. The purpose of the new directive was to prevent the "great losses [which] have heretofore happened by fier"—and specifically, one assumes, the type of fire which takes hold so easily in a roof of thatch. *Ibid.*, 26.

11. This preference seems to have been general throughout the New England colonies, as is evident in any of the still extant buildings from the period, including those at Plymouth. Carson and Candee ("Report on Architecture," 30) note the following specification from a building plan of 1637 at Ipswich, Mass.: "For windowes, let them not be over large in any roome, & few as conceivably may be." (Letter of Samuel Symonds to John Winthrop, Jr., in *Massachusetts Historical Society Collections*, Ser. 4, VII, 118–20.)

cloth or oiled paper,[12] but later glass was more commonly used.[13] By the latter half of the century all of the more substantial houses had the leaded casement windows that were so common at this time in England.

To our own eyes these dwellings would probably have seemed rather dour and forbidding. When viewed from a distance their heavy beams, small windows, and plank or board walls darkened by the weather would have created a massive, brooding kind of effect. In most respects it is easier to see in this housing the lasting influence of medieval style and spirit than any tendency to prefigure later "colonial architecture."

And the interior of an average Plymouth house would have seemed very much of a piece with its outside appearance. With so few windows it must have remained quite dark all the time: perhaps, indeed, in cloudy weather the settlers were obliged to keep candles burning all day. The low ceilings and dark walls would only have intensified the feeling of oppressiveness. But this, of course, speaks only for our own impressions. The settlers themselves were presumably quite content with such houses. For them there was no value in trying to connect their domestic setting with the elemental forces outside. Of sunlight they had plenty, during long days at work in their fields. Of "fresh air" they had likewise more than enough. Their houses seem to imply, and were *meant* to imply, a radical disjunction between the natural and the man-made environments. To them Nature was no long-lost love to be courted and admired at every opportunity. To them, indeed, she frequently presented herself in the guise of antagonist, and they saw no reason to try and make place for her in their homes.

The main room in these single-bay houses was usually called

12. Edward Winslow, in the course of a long letter written for would-be immigrants into the Old Colony, recommended that they "bring paper and linseed oil for your windows." See Heath, *Journal of the Pilgrims,* 86.
13. The first mention of leaded glass among the various Old Colony source materials occurs in 1641. See the inventory of the estate of William Kemp of Duxbury, *Mayflower Descendant,* IV, 81. Subsequently windows of this type are mentioned with some regularity in deeds of sale.

the "hall." Sometimes it was the *only* room, spanning the whole
of the ground-level area. Its dimensions were not, of course, standard, but were normally on the order of fifteen to twenty feet a
side.[14] This seems really rather small, considering the enormous
range of activities that it supported. Access to the hall often involved an entrance porch projecting out from some part of the
house,[15] though occasionally too it was through a door built directly into a wall. The former alternative was presumably more
efficient from the standpoint of heating. A massive chimney stack
and fireplace was the dominant feature of the hall, and indeed of
the whole building. In the earliest phase of Plymouth history
frame-built chimneys daubed with plaster were common, and
there may have been a few stacks made from fieldstones.[16] There
was, however, a subsequent shift to brick chimneys, beginning
somewhat before the middle of the century (and at just the time
when bricklayers are first mentioned in the Colony records).[17]
The typical fireplace of the time seems positively cavernous by
our own standards, but of course it served a much wider range of
needs. A length of seven feet was not uncommon, and the lintel
was usually set three to four feet above the base. Sometimes there
was an oven built into the bricks at the rear of the fireplace.[18]

Recent research on Plymouth architecture has shown that many

14. The dimensions of the Churchill, Howland, and Sparrow houses (all
still extant) were very nearly identical, at least in their original form. They
have recently been measured at approximately 16 feet by 21 feet.
15. As in the Churchill house—which, however, has the unusual feature of
an entryway open to the roof. See Carson and Candee, "Report on Architecture," 9.
16. A "daubed" chimney was specified in a building contract of 1637. *Plymouth Colony Records*, XII, 26. Recent excavations at the site of the John
Howland House have produced some traces of what may have been an old
stone chimney. See James Deetz, "The Howlands of Rocky Nook," Supple-
ment to *The Howland Quarterly*, XXIV, no. 4, 4.
17. Brick chimneys are mentioned in building plans from the early 1640s.
See, for example, *Records of the Town of Plymouth*, I (Plymouth, 1889),
11; and *Plymouth Colony Records*, XII, 26.
18. See, for instance, the reference to a chimney with "an oven therein," in
Plymouth Colony Records, II, 22.

of these single-bay dwellings actually included two rooms on the ground floor.[19] This was managed simply by walling off one end of the hall with clapboards or some other form of planking. The resultant compartment was usually known as an "inner room." Its advantages in terms of privacy and a more efficient division of household functions are self-evident. In England the "inner room" was most often used as a service or storage area; [20] sometimes, in fact, it went by the name of "buttery." But in Plymouth the typical pattern seems to have been somewhat different. From the evidence of the inventories it frequently contained a bed and bedding, and very little more. Occasionally it was the principal bedroom, judging from the presence of a "furnished" or curtained bed.

In most of these story-and-a-half buildings, and in some that had only a single story, there was a loft overhead. Such places were variously described in wills and inventories—sometimes as "upper room," sometimes as "chamber." In virtually all cases they were used for sleeping by some members of the household, though they also served other purposes as we shall see shortly. Access was often by a steep little staircase built flush against the chimney stack. But in some houses there was only a ladder. (Evidence about such architectural details occasionally comes in devious and grisly ways; thus in the records of a murder trial there is testimony by witnesses who saw "at the foot of a ladder which leadeth into an upper chamber, much blood." [21]

The inside walls of these houses were normally covered over with clapboards, or in a few recorded instances with "wainscot." [22] But there was nothing very grand about any of this panelling; the materials and the finish hardly differed from what

19. This is an important outcome of the research of Carson and Candee. See their "Report on Architecture," 11.
20. See M. W. Barley, *The English Farmhouse and Cottage* (London, 1961), 133–34.
21. *Plymouth Colony Records*, II, 133.
22. See *Plymouth Colony Records*, XII, 26; and *ibid.*, 129, 130.

was used on the outside of the building. The settlers did have an advantage over their counterparts in England in one respect: they had real wood floors.[23] It was the growing shortage of timber in the mother country which argued so strongly for earthen or plaster floors, but in the New World, of course, there was no problem on that count.

The third major "type" of Plymouth housing was really just an enlargement of the second. The crucial difference was a ground floor containing two full-size rooms, which were normally set on either side of the chimney.[24] One of these continued to serve as the "hall," while the other was called the "parlor" or "best room." There was less reason here than in the single-bay dwellings to partition off one end of the hall so as to make an "inner room," though clearly nothing prevented such a plan. Overhead there was a corresponding expansion of space. Two upstairs' lofts were common in these houses, and they were usually identified by reference to the rooms below (thus "parlor chamber" and "hall chamber"). Since the chimney was normally in the middle of the house every room might have its own fireplace.

Here, as elsewhere, the notion of fundamental "types" needs some qualification. There is, for example, the matter of chronological sequence. Our discussion has implied that the three kinds of housing formed a series in time, with the second replacing the first, and the third succeeding the second. But this was true only in the most general sense. Clearly there were major areas of overlap in the sequence; the pattern of change was evident strictly in terms of the relative prominence of the various types. At any

---

23. On the English trend to plaster (or earthen) floors, see Barley, *The English Farmhouse and Cottage*, 82–84. For board floors at Plymouth, see various deeds of sale in *Plymouth Colony Records*, XII, 86–87, 111–12, 187, 199.

24. Will Wright's house was apparently of this type. It was inventoried along with the rest of his estate in 1633. See *Mayflower Descendant*, I, 203–5. Likewise, too, the houses of William Kemp (IV, 75–82) and John Atwood (V, 154–57).

given point in time both single and double-bay dwellings could be found in Plymouth, and perhaps some examples of the simple, unframed "cottage" as well.

We must also recognize that all Plymouth housing, of whatever basic design, was likely to be refashioned in one way or another at the discretion of its owner. The most important single variant was the addition of a "lean-to" along the rear of a house.[25] This was a somewhat makeshift structure set right against a wall, with one or two doors providing access from the adjacent ground-floor rooms. An addition to the chimney stack was often possible, permitting the new room to have its own large fireplace. Indeed, in some households the lean-to seems to have become the chief kitchen area. The inventories also suggest, however, that many lean-tos were used mainly for storage—and even for sleeping.[26] Here, then, is another instance of the first principle to be recognized in connection with Plymouth house plans: that the function of given rooms was never fixed or predetermined, that any particular space might be used in several different ways, either successively or even simultaneously. With small houses and large families there was really no alternative.

Lean-tos were not invariably limited to the rear part of Plymouth houses. The Harlow House, one of the few Old Colony dwellings still extant today, is basically a single-bay structure, but it also has two lean-to additions, one at the back and another along its west side. In restoring the house for modern-day visitors, the Plymouth Antiquarian Society has identified the side lean-to as a "scullery" and fitted it out with a cheese press, a butter churn, as-

25. Such lean-tos are mentioned in a number of inventories. See, for example, the estate of John Barnes, published in *The Plymouth Scrap Book*, ed. Charles H. Pope (Boston, 1918), 105.
26. Occasionally a lean-to room is explicitly called a "chamber" (the period word for bedroom). See, for example, the inventory of Ralph Partridge, in Plymouth Probates, II, part 1, folios 67–73. (Registry of Deeds, Plymouth County, Plymouth, Mass.)

sorted mortars and pestles, a supply of herbs and spices, and various pieces of farming equipment. The addition along the rear is more complex, since it is subdivided into three parts. The largest of these is now called the "loom room," in deference to the huge old hand-loom which the restorers have placed along one wall. The two smaller sections are an "inner room" containing a large bed, and a "buttery" filled with all sorts of cooking and eating utensils. The "loom room" cannot be documented in any of the surviving Old Colony records, but otherwise these designations seem reasonable enough. Upstairs there are two regular bedrooms, one substantially larger than the other, plus several small spaces under the eaves. The latter may have been used either for storage or as sleeping areas for some of the younger children of the household. All of this serves to illustrate the degree of complexity possible even within the cramped little framework of the typical seventeenth-century house plan.[27]

In trying to canvass the most familiar variants on the basic forms of Plymouth architecture, we cannot overlook the largest type of building. For the underlying trend throughout the century was towards greater size and greater differentiation. The house of the first William Bradford seems to have contained at least three large ground-floor rooms (though one of them may have been a lean-to extension).[28] In the eighteenth century a four-room floor plan became increasingly common, and it is possible that some dwellings of this type appeared before the end of the Old Colony period. Moreover, houses of full two-story elevation were showing up more and more as time went on. In the inventories for men who owned such houses there is often a reference to a loft or "garret" under the roof. Finally, in most of the larger structures and at least some of the smaller ones, there was a

27. It must be said that the original arrangement of upstairs' rooms was lost when a new, gambrel roof was built sometime in the first half of the eighteenth century. But the current pattern cannot be radically different and may stand in a general way for the seventeenth century as well.
28. See *Mayflower Descendant*, II, 228–34.

cellar of some sort.[29] Usually it did not encompass the full dimensions of the ground-level floor plan, and sometimes it was placed under a lean-to rather than the main part of the house. It was entered either by a descending stairway on the outside, or through a trapdoor in the floor of the room directly overhead.

29. William Kemp's house had a cellar when he died in 1641. See his inventory, in *Mayflower Descendant*, IV, 79. See also the inventories for the estates of John Barnes, in Pope, *Plymouth Scrap Book*, 102–8; and John Attwood, in *Mayflower Descendant*, V, 153–59. Cellars that presumably date from this period can be entered and observed at the Churchill House in Plymouth and the Bradford House in Kingston.

CHAPTER TWO

FURNISHINGS

❧

If, as I hope, the preceding discussion has served to delineate the basic shapes and styles of Old Colony housing, it is time now to add the furnishings. For this subject the inventories represent a virtual encyclopedia of information. The difficulty, indeed, is to know just how to handle such a wealth of specific detail—how to sort it out and how to use it in forming meaningful generalizations.

But there is one point of much importance which emerges from even the most cursory reading of the extant inventories: the households of Plymouth varied along a wide range with respect to the possession of material objects. This should be emphasized at the outset, since in the discussion that follows we are obliged to deal largely with average people and holdings. Moreover, the temptation is strong to think of seventeenth-century communities as broadly homogeneous and undifferentiated. Distinctions of wealth and status form no real part of our traditional picture of the earliest phase of American history.

Yet this impression is badly in need of correction. Perhaps two observations of a very general kind will help to indicate the true shape of the matter. First, the inventories show a clear trend throughout the seventy-year span of Plymouth Colony toward more ample and more diversified physical possessions. This was roughly true for all classes of people; in short, the whole community moved slowly toward greater material prosperity. It also seems, however, that the *distance* between the richest and the poorest citizens widened steadily as the years passed. No one at Plymouth possessed a large amount of personal property in the first decade or so of settlement; distinctions among different households reflected only relative degrees of austerity. But by the middle of the century this situation had changed drastically—as a few specific examples may help to indicate. Web Adey, who has already been mentioned in another context, seems to have stood at the very lowest end of the economic scale. His possessions, as canvassed in 1652, represented an overall value of only £3. 7s.[1] Among the other inventories filed in the same year were those of William Pontus, totalling less than £13 (including £8 for house and lands),[2] and John Ewer, assessed at just over £17.[3] By contrast, the holdings of William Thomas (a "gentleman" of Marshfield) were valued a few months earlier at some £375.[4] His "wearing apparrell" alone was worth more than the entire estates of Adey, Pontus, or Ewer; and his "plate" (that is, silver table utensils) represented a greater value than all the properties of the other three put together.

These contrasts appear still more striking in relation to specific kinds of possessions. The poorest families, for example, seem to have done without any sort of table linen. Yet the linens belonging to "Mistress Ann Attwood" would look incredibly extensive even

1. *Mayflower Descendant*, XI, 8.
2. *Ibid.*, 92–94.
3. *Ibid.*, 10–11.
4. *Mayflower Descendant*, X, 162–64.

against the pattern of our own day. Her estate, as reported just after her death in 1654, included no less than eighteen tablecloths and sixty-six napkins! [5] Holdings such as this reflect certain broader concepts of value that were standard among the first generations of settlers. Presumably Mrs. Attwood did not try to make regular use of all her table linen in the everyday course of her life at Plymouth. (Nor, for that matter, did she often use each of her fifteen pairs of bedsheets, eight petticoats, and forty odd handkerchiefs.) Instead, she kept them—probably locked up in chests—as a form of "capital." There was relatively little money circulating in the Old Colony, and there certainly were no banks in which to deposit savings. Thus wealth necessarily implied some tangible kind of investment. The possession of land was obviously desirable on this account, since the overall trend in land values was upward throughout the century. But another alternative, and perhaps an even safer one, was investment in some of the basic artifacts of domestic life. This was especially true for objects that had to be imported from overseas—objects, in short, whose value was not subject to sudden changes in local patterns of production. Mrs. Attwood's "silke mohear petticoat" (worth nearly £2), her "2 silver beerbowles," her "great bible," and even her "velvett muffe" can all be recognized as properties that were not likely to depreciate over time. They may or may not have performed regular service in her household. But in any case they represented a good investment, a sound way of preserving and demonstrating her personal wealth.

Ann Attwood and Web Adey clearly present extreme cases of domestic life, revealing little that is relevant to the great majority of Old Colony households. [6] Let us try, therefore, to make a brief

5. The entire inventory is published in *Mayflower Descendant*, XI, 201–6.
6. The narrative which follows represents an amalgam of my own impressions, as formed from an extensive reading among the extant inventories from the Old Colony period, and the conclusions of certain specialists in the historical study of domestic furnishings. Miss Rose Briggs, curator of the Plymouth Antiquarian Society, spent an afternoon instructing me in the use of many objects currently on display either at Pilgrim Hall in Plymouth

mind's-eye canvass of an average home, defining the term "average" for the moment as the type of single-bay, story-and-a-half dwelling discussed some pages earlier. The "hall" is the right place to begin, since it was there that so many of the essential operations of family life took place. By our own standards the typical hall of the seventeenth century would have seemed a jumbled, confusing place. Cooking, eating, spinning, sewing, carpentry, prayer, schooling, entertaining, and even sleeping were among the activities that it regularly supported; and each one demanded its own set of props. The need for some degree of orderliness and efficiency must have required constant attention to the disposition of objects in this room, but there is no reason to imagine any set principles common to every household. Indeed, the objects themselves imply an opposite tendency—a kind of easy flexibility, a willingness to improvise whenever necessary in order to make the best use of available space. The first consideration was to have ready access to those objects which were needed in the performance of any given task—and to keep the others more or less out of the way. It seems likely, therefore, that most of the furnishings in a typical hall were set close against the walls, leaving a large central area free as working space. But this is only speculation; it is the kind of thing which cannot be finally verified.

The one important structural factor bearing on the arrangement of the hall was the position of the fireplace. Surely most of the essential cooking utensils were concentrated here or very close by. The interior of the hearth itself appeared extremely cluttered and complicated; it contained a veritable maze of wrought-iron accoutrements. Suspended from the "lug pole" at the mouth of the

<hr />

or at the Harlow House. I consulted two unpublished papers on the subject: Richard B. Bailey, "Pilgrim Possessions—1620–1640" (on file at Plimoth Plantation); and Flora Tachau, "Early New England Colonial Life" (on file at Pilgrim Hall). George Francis Dow, *Everyday Life in the Massachusetts Bay Colony* (Boston, 1935) also proved useful (since the range of household objects common at this time differed very little between the two neighbor colonies).

chimney were a variety of hooks and bars and chains. Andirons rose from the base, and out along the sides were the tools used in the actual handling of fire (shovels, tongs, forks, and bellows). Other objects commonly associated with the fireplace included warming pans, foot stoves, brooms, and perhaps a small "pipe box" (where the master of the house would keep his pipes and tobacco). Some of these accessories were more important than others; and it was only the wealthier families that possessed anything like the full complement.

It is equally difficult to offer precise generalizations about the equipment directly involved in cooking, for once again the inventories show a wide range of possibilities. James Cushman (whose estate was reported in 1648) seems to present a kind of bottom case, with just "one smale iron pott," "a smale scillite," and "one smale brass scimer." [7] But Cushman belonged to the poorest class of citizens, and furthermore he seems not to have been married. In that case he may possibly have lived as part of some joint household—either with other single men or as a kind of "boarder" in a family. Perhaps, in short, he did not need to have in his own possession even a minimum set of kitchen utensils. The estate of William Palmer (filed in 1637) falls much closer in this regard to some overall norm.[8] Palmer ranked near the middle of the Colony's economic scale, and he was also a family man. His belongings included the following: "11 iron potts, 1 great Kettle, 4 kettles 2 old & 2 new, 1 bakeing pan, 1 skellet, 1 scummer, 11 frying panns, 1 iron ladle, 1 spitt, and 1 driping pan."

Despite the vagaries of seventeenth-century spelling, most of these listings are recognizable in terms of our own domestic *equipage*. The "scummer" (spelled "scimer" in Cushman's inventory, or "skimmer" as we would render it) was for removing floating materials from the top of a potful of food. Ladles served a similar

7. *Mayflower Descendant*, IX, 82.
8. *Mayflower Descendant*, II, 148–52.

purpose and were also helpful in basting. Dripping pans caught the runoff from roasting meat. The Palmers seem not to have owned a number of other utensils that are sometimes listed elsewhere. Among these were "trivets" or tripods for supporting cauldrons and pots over the open fire; gridirons; the mortars and pestles commonly used in pounding corn and other foods; the "posnet" (a kind of saucepan, often constructed with its own set of legs); and the "slice" (a spatula used for moving bread or meat in and out of the fireplace and oven). Much of this cookware seems rather crudely made, but it was extremely sturdy and sometimes served a family through two or three generations. Blackened by long use, and made from heavy materials, it presents today a most ponderous appearance. One important concession to convenience was the construction of long handles on some of these articles (skillets, ladles, and skimmers). But all things considered, cooking under seventeenth-century conditions must have involved a great deal of arduous lifting and reaching.

This roster of utensils employed around the fireplace by no means exhausts the full range of equipment connected with the care and preparation of food. The settlers had to perform for themselves a variety of services now left to commercial enterprise; thus their inventories show some objects with which we are not so familiar. For instance, there were butter churns, cheese presses, salt barrels, and "keelers" (a sort of shallow basin frequently used in cooling liquids). But these were fairly bulky items and would not normally occupy space in the hall. More frequently, it seems, they were relegated to a shed behind the main building—or, in larger houses, to a buttery or scullery.

The hall was not only a kitchen but a dining room as well. However, the accessories used in this connection were very modest, in keeping with the need to make the best use of limited space. The dining table was often nothing more than a couple of planks set on trestles. For seating there were simple benches to be drawn up on either side, with perhaps a single chair placed at one end for the use of the head of the household.[9] When a meal was over, the whole arrangement could be quickly dismantled for storage in a corner or against a wall.

Most households had at least a limited quantity of table linen: a cloth or two to lay over the surface, and a number of simple napkins. (Some people, as previously noted, had a great deal more than this.) Among eating utensils, spoons were the one essential item.[10] Knives turned up much more rarely, and forks were nonexistent. Most utensils were made from some metal alloy, though as time passed silver began to appear, especially in the homes of the well-to-do.[11] Dishes came in various shapes, sizes, and materials. Platters or "trenchers" made of wood were standard among people of limited means; earthenware was fairly common, and also pewter. For liquids there were beakers, bowls, and cups—again available in any of several different materials. Sometimes one of these containers sufficed for a whole family and was passed from hand to hand as a meal progressed. The inventories also record a number of saltcellars, and miscellaneous bottles (made more often of pewter than of glass). How this tableware was stored we cannot be sure. In the more affluent households it probably occupied a specific part of a pantry room or was arranged as a ceremonial display in the parlor. In poorer ones it was likely set in or atop a chest, box, or bench.

Among the larger furnishings found in a typical hall the most important were the chests. Since none of these seventeenth-century houses had closets, portable chests (and "boxes" and

9. It may be that in some households people stood up to eat—especially children.
10. Spoons are one of the most common items recovered in current excavation work at Old Colony sites. Plimoth Plantation has a large store of them in its archaeological collections.
11. Thus, for example, William Kemp's inventory (of 1641) shows "10 silver spoones," "1 jugg pott tipt wth silvr," and "1 cup tipt wth silver." And the inventory of Mistress Ann Attwood (1654) lists spoons, beer bowls, wine cups, saltcellars, and dishes—all in silver.

"trunks") provided the chief facilities for storage. Their importance was enhanced by the fact that they could also serve as seats or tables. All in all they seem to have been one of the truly indispensable articles of furniture in this time. A "box" was a much smaller type of object. Whereas chests might hold clothing, bedding, or large tools, boxes were customarily used for keeping spices, buttons, nails, thread, and the like.[12] In some homes there was a "Bible box"—that is, a special container set on a table to hold a Bible or something else of particular value.

Tables and chairs were present in most Old Colony households, but in rather limited numbers. Indeed, a single full-fledged chair seems to have sufficed in many cases, and it was probably reserved for older people. There was also, however, a variety of simple stools and "forms" (benches) to accommodate the other members of the family. Once again the pattern was substantially different in the wealthier households; thus, for example, there was as early as 1633 one estate which included a total of *five* chairs.[13] Tables were still less common, and presumably less important too, since the values attributed to them were generally quite small. Occasionally in the inventories one finds a carpet listed together with a table—a reminder that in the period we are describing carpets were used not on the floor but for covering various raised surfaces.

The hall might well contain one or more bedsteads. This obviously tightened the squeeze on the limited space that was available there, but in large families it was sometimes a plain necessity. The earliest bedsteads were simply a length of cord laced back and forth between the sides of a rough wooden frame. Later on, there are references to headboards and even to "hanging bedsteads" (elaborate structures with tall posts and fitted to hold curtains all around). The settlers used the word "beds" (as opposed

12. Both chests and boxes, of various shapes and sizes, can be seen in the display at Pilgrim Hall.
13. See the inventory of Samuel Fuller, Plymouth Probates, I, part 1, folio 22. (Registry of Deeds, Plymouth County, Plymouth, Mass.)

to the bed*steads* already described) to refer to what we would call mattresses. And they came in many different forms. "Feather beds" were usually a mark of wealth; in fact, the inventories show them to have been among the most valuable of all household possessions.[14] "Flock beds" represented a much more modest alternative. The term was a kind of catchall for various sorts of bag mattresses stuffed with rags, bits of wool, or any other odd materials that were ready at hand. Sheets are rather widely distributed through the inventories, as are pillows, "pillow beers" (cases or covers), and blankets. "Rugs" are also mentioned occasionally as bedding, indicating, it seems, coverings that were heavier than ordinary blankets. "Coverlets," or spreads, appear chiefly in the estates of the wealthy, and the same is true of bed curtains. (For those who could afford them, curtained beds had clear advantages in terms of both warmth and privacy.) The range of possibilities here has been summarized as follows by a previous student of Old Colony furnishings: "An early Plymouth bed might have been anything from a simple flock bed on the ground to a bedstead with a feather bed and bolster, pillow, pillow case, sheets, blankets, rugs, coverlets, curtains, and a warming pan standing nearby." [15]

There is one final point about seventeenth-century beds—and an important one, since it shows the spirit of improvisation and flexibility so characteristic of all the domestic arrangements of the period. Some of the bedsteads were joined at one end, by hinges, to a wall. This meant that when not in use they could be turned up and put completely out of the way. Another, comparable device was the so-called "trundle-bed," in which a full-size frame was superimposed on a smaller one. The latter was of course for young children, and at night it was pulled out for regular use.

14. The precise value of "feather beds" naturally varied somewhat, depending on the quality and condition of any particular example thereof; but the average was roughly £3. This was equivalent to the value of a young cow or a full set of kitchen equipment.
15. See Bailey, "Pilgrim Possessions," 4.

But in the daytime it could easily be tucked away under its "parent." Here, then, is one more instance of the effort to save on floor space.

The hall was the setting for certain types of household manufacture, and its furnishings reflected this fact too. Wheels for spinning were certainly important, though judging from the inventories they were not found widely among the settlers until after the middle of the century. Weaving looms were much more complicated, bulky, and expensive, and cannot reasonably be attributed to the average household in any period. Some families made their own candles and possessed a set of molds for the purpose; others had equipment for producing tableware. Then, too, some of the things that were normally used outdoors found their way into the hall—saws, and hoes, and especially guns.

Our catalogue of the furnishings likely in a seventeenth-century hall has necessarily been a long one, since this room was so clearly the locus of all essential household activities. But the task of surveying the other rooms is correspondingly simplified. The "inner room" normally held just a bed, a chest, and possibly a few random articles set in a corner so as to be temporarily out of the way.[16] The loft overhead was also quite sparsely furnished. Beds were certainly standard there, perhaps another chest, and in a few instances a chair or bench. There is also much evidence for the use of this area as storage space. Thus, for example, Will Wright's inventory (filed in 1633) shows a loft filled with axes, chisels, saws, knives, hoes, fishing tackle, barrels, and "other lumber of small value."[17] One feature of seventeenth-century architecture, not previously mentioned, may also have a bearing on this practice. It

16. The inventory of Thomas Lapham, for example, shows the contents of his "inner room" to have been: a trundle bed, three chests, a trunk, two boxes, a bedpan, 17 pairs of sheets, and three pillow cases. *Mayflower Descendant*, X, 199. As an example of another pattern—i.e. with a much wider range of objects placed there—see the pertinent section of the inventory of William Kemp. *Mayflower Descendant*, IV, 75 ff.

17. *Mayflower Descendant*, I, 205.

appears that in some Plymouth houses the upstairs floorboards were left unfastened to any joist or beam.[18] Thus they could be readily removed whenever it was necessary to transfer heavy articles to and from the loft—and surely there were times when this seemed a welcome boon.

One general conclusion about Old Colony households should now be transparently clear: No room apart from the hall was furnished so as to imply regular use by the residents in their normal round of waking activities. Almost certainly the central consideration here was the problem of heating. There are in New England six or seven months each year when some degree of artificial heat is quite necessary. (In the dead of winter, of course, the situation becomes extreme for weeks on end.) The colonists thus depended heavily on their hall fireplaces for keeping warm. Some houses, to be sure, were built with a second hearth upstairs, but probably under normal circumstances it seemed extravagant to keep two fires going at the same time.

If these details of architecture and furnishings seem rather arid in themselves, they nonetheless have profound implications for some of the more intangible aspects of family life. Consider especially the question of privacy, and indeed the whole area of relations among the different members of a household. It is commonplace nowadays to decry the erosion of personal privacy under the impact of various trends in modern life—the growth of cities, the mass media, the whole ethos of "organization," and above all the sheer increase in human population. Yet this picture is badly distorted, for it lacks any true historical perspective. It fails, moreover, to recognize the most intimate of all the basic theaters of human interaction—the home. The fact is that we in our homes of the mid-twentieth century have more privacy, more actual living

18. In 1650 the widow Mary Paddock sold her house complete with "boards both loose and nailed." *Plymouth Colony Records*, XII, 199. But other transactions specifically excluded the floorboards from a sale. *Ibid.*, 26, 86–87, 111–12.

space *per capita*, than any previous generation in history. The contrast with the situation that confronted the people of Plymouth, or indeed of any seventeenth-century community, can be most instructive. It is not just that their houses were small to begin with. It is not just that even within this limited space a considerable part was used only for sleeping and storage. It is not just that their families were large, much more so than our own.[19] It is not just that their ordinary activities were confined to a small radius in and around the home. It is rather the *combination of all these factors* that we must try somehow to grasp. Can we picture ourselves in such a setting—as one of a group of five, six, eight, or even a dozen people living and working and playing all together, day after day, in one room of rather modest size? One might ask, in fact, whether privacy would then be a meaningful concept at all.

Our discussion has so far been tied to the single-bay, story-and-a-half dwelling, since this was the closest thing to "average" housing in the Old Colony period. Still the larger units merit at least a little direct consideration. To what extent must the picture formed above be modified so as to fit houses with two or more main rooms on each floor? It is clear, first of all, that greater size, the addition of more rooms, created some tendency toward the separation of the various domestic functions.[20] This was most obviously so in the case of separate kitchens: when all the tasks involved in preparing food were consigned to a room of their own, the situation in the hall was greatly simplified. Similarly, when a second large room downstairs was set up as a "parlor," a new sort of division became likely among the different kinds of personal property attached to the household. The parlor was sometimes

19. See below, pp. 64, 68.
20. For discussion of similar questions with reference to English households of the sixteenth and seventeenth centuries, see W. G. Hoskins, "The Rebuilding of Rural England, 1570–1640," first published in *Past and Present*, no. 4 (1953); and reprinted in his *Provincial England* (London, 1963), 131–48.

known also by the term "best room," and it was usually the place where the family kept their "best" and most valuable possessions. Apparently its use was limited to special circumstances and occasions, such as the entertainment of important guests, though there is also evidence in some cases that it was the room in which the master and mistress of the household slept.[21] In a sense, then, its function was mostly ceremonial; but even this represents a real step away from the highly undifferentiated style of living characteristic of the smaller houses. A further elaboration of this trend was the creation of different rooms (that is, *bed*rooms) for different members of the family; but this lay wholly beyond the seventeenth century.

In sum, the gradual increase in the average size of houses in the Old Colony foreshadowed major realignments in a whole network of human relationships. Still it was many years before these changes were fully realized. Even within the larger houses of Plymouth the hall was the vital center for most domestic activities. Men and women, children and adults moved constantly among and around one another in the pursuit of their various objectives. The limited space available was arranged and rearranged, divided and subdivided, so as to achieve at any given moment the best possible accommodation of the interests of all concerned. Perhaps there were some explicit agreements and "rules" defining appropriate behavior under these circumstances, but surely the most important factor of all in making the situation work was the force of unconscious habit. The necessities of the matter were all too obvious and were communicated wordlessly—even, one assumes, to very young children. Countless little episodes each day confirmed the importance of creative adjustments in the use of space.

But while most people "managed," or even "succeeded," in

21. As, for example, in the household of William Bradford. Note the contents of his parlor, as listed in the inventory of his estate, in *Mayflower Descendant*, II, 228–34.

making these adjustments, was there no cost, no hardship in terms more intimate and personal than anything we have considered so far? If one accepts with most of modern psychology that every man harbors both loving *and* hostile impulses of a very basic kind, what of the latter under the conditions of life that prevailed in seventeenth-century Plymouth? How, in particular, did these cramped little households avoid an atmosphere of constant bickering and recrimination? We cannot, of course, be absolutely sure that they *did* avoid such an atmosphere, but there is little evidence left to suggest any unusual degree of family tensions. The Court Records contain a relatively modest number of cases reflecting conflict within a particular family, and this is all the more striking in a community that invested its public authorities with official jurisdiction over a very broad range of domestic matters.[22] The Records also show, however, an enormous quantity of actions between neighbors. By far the greatest portion of these were disputes over property, but often too they revealed a deep strain of personal antagonism. Cases of debt or trespass were sometimes directly coupled with charges of slander and battery.[23]

If we bring together these two bodies of data—the few recorded cases of conflict within a family, and the very many such cases among neighbors—there appears the germ of an hypothesis which may be worth an explicit statement. The word "hypothesis" should be stressed here, since this is not something which can be verified by the methods most familiar to historical scholarship. But the issue involved is a telling one: namely, the way people learn to handle their own feelings of anger and aggression.[24] The cramped conditions in which the settlers were obliged to live have

22. See below, Conclusion.
23. See, for example, the complicated set of legal proceedings involving William Randall and Humphrey Johnson, *Plymouth Colony Records*, I, 110 ff. Also Thomas Summers vs. John Williams, *ibid.*, 122, 125, 138–39; and William Randall vs. Jeremy Hatch and John Turner, *ibid.*, 116–18.
24. See below, Chapter Nine, for a fuller discussion of Puritan attitudes toward anger and aggression.

already been described in considerable detail. It remains only to emphasize the importance of the family as *the primary unit* in virtually all phases of seventeenth-century life. (More of this later on.) [25] In short, the family had to maintain a smooth kind of operational equilibrium; basic disruptions and discontinuities must be avoided at all costs. What this probably meant in practice was a strong unconscious restraint on the expression of hostile impulses against the members of one's own household.

To call this restraint "unconscious" is not to imply that it was easy to maintain, or that family life under these conditions reflected some natural tendency towards inner harmony. Formal restraints could, of course, also be applied when necessary and appropriate—particularly with the very young.[26] Firm discipline was a touchstone of household organization in this culture, though after childhood it was a process largely internal (that is, *self*-discipline). In either case it imposed a cost in terms of energy and effort. Domestic peace, in short, was achieved only with an element of real struggle.

But it seems that *occasions* for abrasive contact must have been there aplenty, and the anger that resulted had to find some outlet in behavior. This is the point at which the field of neighborly relations derives a real, if somewhat sinister, significance. Chronic hostility among neighbors obviously created problems in its own right; but all things considered, this was preferable to the same condition within the sphere of the family. The process is one that psychologists know by the clinical term "displacement." But there is nothing very extraordinary about it. It appears indeed in the life of virtually every individual and every society. We are all occasionally confronted with impulses which, while rooted deep within us, are not acceptable in some given context. Displacement represents a rather simple way of resolving such conflicts. At its worst, it can generate the most vicious kind of scapegoating. But

25. See below, Conclusion.
26. See below, pp. 100–102, 134–36.

in other instances it may serve a purpose which is largely con-
structive in the long run. And such, perhaps, was the typical case
in Plymouth—when a man cursed his neighbor in order to keep
smiling at his parent, spouse, or child.

CHAPTER THREE

CLOTHING

꧁꧂

To complete our picture of the physical environment we need to form some impression of the settlers themselves as they went about their daily business. Here again the inventories are a rich lode of evidence; indeed a number of scholars have already mined them intensively in connection with the study of seventeenth-century clothing.[1] On the other hand, a different sort of evidence is lamentably absent: portraits, or indeed any form of visual representation, created by people who actually lived in that period. Thus we can form sure notions of the contents of a typical wardrobe, but must rely largely on inference when trying to understand how and when the clothes were worn. We are able, as it were, to open the chests and trunks in which the settlers kept their clothes, but the task of trying to "dress" them for any particular occasion is much more problematical.

1. Most of the source material for the study of clothing among the residents of the Old Colony is in the relevant parts of their inventories. A few actual pieces of clothing have survived and may be seen at Pilgrim Hall. I have also consulted an unpublished essay by Rose Briggs, "Pilgrim Dress," on file at Pilgrim Hall.

One overall conclusion which seems beyond reasonable doubt concerns the matter of range and variety. The clothing in common use among the settlers was surprisingly diverse—in types of articles, in materials employed, in methods of manufacture, and in recognized values. Clothes, like household furnishings, represented "money in the bank"; hence many of the wealthier people accumulated them in extremely large quantities.[2] We know too that in this culture clothing was always an important measure of status—what a man wore reflected his worth in the eyes of his neighbors. In fact, the government of the Massachusetts Bay Colony worked out a set of legal regulations about the garments admissible for each class of men.[3] No such laws existed in Plymouth, but the force of public opinion probably acted with similar effect. In any case the same underlying assumptions must have been generally prevalent in the Old Colony, and they provide a second part of the explanation for the great disparity in the wardrobes typical of rich and poor citizens. In short, clothing was not only a good investment for a man of some means; it was also a way of demonstrating his standing in the larger community and of confirming his own self-image.

Several further observations of a fairly general kind are in order. The matter of color has been badly distorted in some traditional accounts of Puritan and Pilgrim dress. We tend to think that austere combinations of black and white framed the limits of accepted practice for these people, but the inventories clearly suggest otherwise. It is true that black carried certain connotations of dignity and formality and thus was standard for many sorts of "best clothes" (worn on Sundays or other ceremonial occasions). Daily garb, however, was another story; here a broad spectrum of colors was tolerated, and even assumed. "Russet," or various

2. William Bradford, for one, had a wardrobe of astonishing size and diversity. See *Mayflower Descendant*, II, 228–34. See also Mistress Ann Attwood, *Mayflower Descendant*, XI, 201–6.
3. *The Records of the Governor and Company of the Massachusetts Bay in New England*, ed. Nathaniel B. Shurtleff, 5 vols. (Boston, 1853–54), I, 126.

shades of orange-brown, seems to have been the most common choice; but the inventories also show many items in red, blue, green, yellow, purple, and so forth. In general, the color range of this period would seem rather soft if compared directly with our own—reflecting the difference in tone between vegetable and chemical dyes.

But if the settlers accepted color as a normal facet of their dress, they rejected certain other forms of more manifest display: they were not, after all, Puritans for nothing. Jewelry was disapproved, and the women of Plymouth, like Puritan women everywhere, did not even wear wedding rings.[4] They also avoided the elaborate ruffs and headdresses, the sharply pointed bodices, the billowing farthingale skirts, which were fashionable among the genteel classes in England at this time.[5]

The fabrics used in making their garments comprised many variants of wool, linen, and leather. Serge, flannel, fustian, Holland, buckram, kersey, linsey-woolsey, lockram—the names run literally into the dozens and form a terminology far more extensive than the comparable parts of common usage today. There are areas, it seems, in which the "simple" life of our forbears reveals a complexity, a range of subtle shadings and distinctions, which has not been equalled in any recent period. Cotton, incidentally, was still an expensive material in the seventeenth century and turned up only rarely in the wardrobes of Plymouth.

Most of these fabrics were quite heavy and durable, and thus clothes could be expected to last for many years. Some items descended through two or even three generations—which indeed is why the inventories are such a good source for the study of dress. Their value in sheer monetary terms was often quite substantial, particularly in the case of things not produced in the colonies. A fine suit for a man, or the best kind of woman's petticoat, might

4. Briggs, "Pilgrim Dress," 2.
5. *Ibid.*, 2-3. On the fashions prevailing in England during the same period see C. W. Cunnington and Phillis Cunnington, *Handbook of English Costume in the Seventeenth Century* (London, 1955).

cost as much as one pound, ten shillings. At the rates that pre-vailed around 1650 this sum would also have bought a young steer, or half a dozen goats, or a complete set of armor, or ten bushels of wheat.

The most common items of dress specific to each sex may now be briefly catalogued; let us start with the women. The outermost garment was a "gown" of some type. Normally, it consisted of three separate parts: a skirt, a bodice, and a pair of sleeves which were tied into the bodice armholes and covered by shoulder pieces called "wings." The skirt was sometimes open at the front to save on wear and tear, revealing a special underskirt made of heavy linen. Petticoats figured as still another layer. Often, indeed, they served in lieu of underskirts and were correspondingly ornate. Be-neath the bodice there was usually some sort of chemise. And finally there were "smocks," loose linen shifts worn next to the skin—in short, the essential item of women's underwear in this period. The inventories also show a considerable number of "aprons," which presumably were put on over the gowns (per-haps as an alternative to an "underskirt").

Many older discussions of seventeenth-century dress have sug-gested that all of these different articles were worn at the same time—comprising no less than five layers on any given occasion. Yet this is most difficult to believe. Perhaps during the winter there was some tendency to pile on several garments in the inter-ests of warmth, but surely not at other times of the year. It is easier to think that the various types of clothing were worn in a range of combinations—gown and apron, petticoat and gown, and so forth. The New England summer has plenty of hot days, and the settlers could not have stuck rigidly to a single pattern of dress.

For their feet the women of Plymouth had leather shoes and various sorts of stockings. Over their shoes they often wore "clogs"—half slippers with thick wooden soles—to protect against mud. Still another common item was the "kerchief," worn around the neck to prevent the upper part of the gown from becoming too soiled. And atop their heads the women invariably wore a linen cap or "coif." Their hair, which was usually bunched tightly together at the back, was in this way almost completely covered. It was thought quite immodest in this society for a woman to go about with her head bared, even within the confines of her own home.

"Best clothes"—appropriate for Sundays or other solemn occasions—did not differ dramatically from the everyday wear sketched above. They were, on the whole, a little finer and a little more well-preserved; and there was less variety of color, more tendency toward the use of black. The typical gown might perhaps be embellished with ruffs at the neck and wrists. A "stomacher" might be added beneath the bodice, and a black felt hat over the cap. But the overall effect was still sober and restrained; the aspect of conscious decorative display was very much muted.

The same general situation obtained with regard to the dress of the men. Functional considerations were equally prominent, and ornamental ones were definitely played down. The inventories suggest that "suits" were perhaps the single most important item. The meaning of the term is indicated by the listing, "one suit being a doublet, cloak, and breeches." [6] But if these were the standard pieces in a suit, it is clear that there was much variety in materials, color, and worth. Wool, canvas, and leather (even "moose leather") are all represented in the inventories, and the range of assigned values is from a few shillings to nearly two pounds. The doublet was a close-fitting jacket, usually worn with wings at the shoulders. Breeches were quite full and ended just below the knee. The cloak was normally of about three-quarter length. Each of these items, incidentally, also appeared separately in many instances. There were other garments, more or less similar to the doublet, for the upper part of the body: most notably, the "jerkin," which was often made from some specially heavy

6. See Bailey, "Pilgrim Possessions," 6.

material and worn on the outside in cold weather, and also the "waistcoat." Men, like women, might sometimes wear several layers of clothing at once—waistcoat, doublet, jerkin and cloak —but not as a regular practice.

The innermost garment was some type of linen shirt. Long stockings (of either wool or linen) were normally covered by "boothose" made from a particularly heavy type of canvas material. Boots were the usual footwear; typically they were of some pliable leather and laced from ankle to calf to ensure a comfortable fit. Caps were not obligatory for men (as they were for women), but seem to have been common nonetheless. A man's "best clothes" were largely a more elegant version of his everyday costume. The only clear differences were at the top and bottom: a black felt hat (with a special "band") on his head, and black shoes instead of boots for his feet.

Something must also be said about the clothing of children in the Old Colony. The inventories are of very little use here, and the antiquarians who have worked hardest on the subject of dress have for the most part been obliged to extrapolate from what is known of the pattern that prevailed in other parts of the colonies and in Europe.[7] However, there is no reason to doubt their central conclusion that children were clothed very much in the manner of their parents.[8] Breeches, shirt, and doublet were almost certainly the standard items for young boys; and cap, chemise, bodice, petticoat and skirt for girls. These are facts whose significance extends well beyond the immediate sartorial context. Indeed they imply a whole view of human life and development substantially different from anything that obtains in our own culture today. Childhood as such was barely recognized in the period

7. See especially Alice M. Earle, *Child Life in Colonial Days* (New York, 1927), 35 ff. Also Briggs, "Pilgrim Dress," 4–5.
8. The most striking kind of evidence here comes from paintings either of individual children or of family groups. See Briggs, "Pilgrim Dress," 4–5. For a full discussion of European portraiture bearing on this question see Philippe Aries, *Centuries of Childhood*, trans. Robert Baldick (New York, 1962), ch. 3.

spanned by Plymouth Colony. There was little sense that children might somehow be a special group, with their own needs and interests and capacities. Instead they were viewed largely as miniature adults: the boy was a little model of his father, likewise the girl of her mother. This point will merit further discussion later on; for now let us note its particular relevance to the matter of dress. In no other way was the continuity of childhood and the later stages of life quite so clearly symbolized.

PART TWO

THE STRUCTURE OF
THE HOUSEHOLD

It is time now to shift our focus to the people who actually formed and maintained these Old Colony households. We must try to discover some of the more significant themes and regularities in their immediate human environment. Questions of the most basic sort arise at once: What categories of people usually comprised a single household? Was there much variation from this standard? What were the terms under which these people lived and loved and worked with one another? Were there prescribed roles and statuses which helped to determine the day-to-day functioning of the household?

These are, of course, extremely elusive questions, and we have no physical remains to allow us to begin with even a false sense of "certainty." Still, some valuable resources do exist, if only the right use can be made of them. There are, to begin with, the laws of the colony, and specifically, the small but significant part of those laws which bear directly on matters of family life. There are also actions which violated the laws. Here, as so often in the investigation of historical materials, it is the unusual or deviant act which we are able most fully to scrutinize. The broad and basic norms of the community are noted barely, if at all; yet their essential shape can often be reconstructed by a process of inference from the record of "abnormal" events and circumstances. The exception does in such cases help very much to "prove the rule."

Moreover, there is a huge corpus of materials reflecting the dealings of these communities with regard to property. In some simple societies, and many complex ones, themes of family and property are deeply intertwined. The family is, indeed, the primary agency for owning, and using, and distributing property. And conversely, considerations of property serve in large measure to determine the specific character of family life—both its outer form, and its inner dynamics. All of this was profoundly true of the early New England communities; hence wills, land deeds, deeds of inheritance and gift will prove of great interest to us. The Plymouth settlers, in particular, had a vivid personal experience bearing out the importance of these relationships, for during their first years in the New World they operated under an essentially communal system of ownership. Bradford's account of the experiment, and of the reasons for its failure, is most illuminating. "This community," he writes, "was found to breed much confusion and discontent and retard much employment that would have been to their benefit and comfort. For the young men, that were most able and fit for labour and service, did repine that they should spend their time and strength to work for other men's wives and children without any recompense. . . . And for men's wives to be commanded to do service for other men, as dressing their meat, washing their clothes, etc., they deemed it a kind of slavery, neither could many husbands well brook it." The remedy for these problems was simply to restore a degree of private ownership—and, in effect, to re-establish the connection between family and property. The authorities "gave way that they should set corn every man for his own particular . . . and so assigned to every family a parcel of land . . . This had very good success, for it made all hands very industrious." [1]

1. William Bradford, *Of Plymouth Plantation*, ed. Samuel Eliot Morison (New York, 1952), 120–21.

CHAPTER FOUR

MEMBERSHIP

❧❦

Recent studies of colonial family life have sought to clear away some serious misconceptions about the size and membership of the typical household. It used to be thought that the norm was some sort of "extended family"—that is, a large assemblage of persons spanning several generations and a variety of kinship connections, all gathered under one roof. The change to our own "nuclear" pattern, with parents and children living apart from all other relatives, was in this view associated with the coming of the Industrial Revolution. It is now apparent, however, that small and essentially nuclear families were standard from the very beginning of American history, and probably from a still earlier time in the history of Western Europe.[1] The evidence for Plymouth is very much in line with these conclusions.

Our survey of Old Colony architecture surely implies some limits on the size of individual families: it is difficult to picture really

1. On this point see Peter Laslett and John Harrison, "Clayworth and Cogenhoe," in H. E. Bell and R. L. Ollard, *Historical Essays, Presented to David Ogg* (London, 1963), 157–84. See also Peter Laslett, *The World We Have Lost* (New York, 1965), 89 ff.

large numbers of people managing to live together in such relatively modest houses. Such a situation might be conceivable in a warm climate, where most of life could be carried on outdoors —but certainly not in New England.

The various deeds of gift and inheritance speak much more directly to the same point. They show beyond any possibility of reasonable doubt that one married couple and their own children always formed the core of the family—and often comprised its entire extent. There were, to be sure, some significant variants on this pattern, but probably no more than can be found in our own day. The most crucial single datum confirmed by the deeds is a clear assumption on all sides that married siblings would never belong to the same household. Contracts made between the families of a prospective bride and groom regularly provided for the building (or purchase) of a separate house for the new couple. The arrangements for the wedding of Joseph Buckland and Deborah Allen of Rehoboth apparently were typical: Buckland's father promised to "build the said Joseph a Convenient house for his Comfortable liveing with three score acrees of land ajoyning to it." [2] Many of the wills reveal a similar pattern. A man invariably left his house to some *one* of his sons—never to more than one. At the same time he sought to provide for the day when his other sons would marry and would need to establish their own separate residences. So, for example, John Washburn of Bridgewater left a special bequest for a younger son "toward his building" [3]—the other children were already living in houses of their own. William Carpenter of Rehoboth, while making his first son (Samuel) his chief heir, did not forget his second one (Abiah). Samuel and Carpenter's widow were specially directed to "healp . . . [Abiah] to build an house; because Samuell hath an house built alreddy." [4] In all of the extant wills there is only one that proposes any kind of

2. *Mayflower Descendant*, XVI, 82.
3. *Mayflower Descendant*, XV, 250.
4. *Mayflower Descendant*, XIV, 231.

joint residence among different married couples, and it clearly recognizes the unusual and temporary nature of such arrangements.
Thomas Bliss of Plymouth, who died in 1647, left his "house and
home lot" to his son Jonathan, on the condition that he assist a
certain son-in-law in building a separate residence and in the
meanwhile "let him peacably and quietly live in the house with
him untell they shall bee able to set up a house for him." [5]

There is one more piece of evidence to introduce at this point: a
rare and extremely valuable census for the town of Bristol, compiled in February, 1689.[6] The arrangement of the census is in itself significant. At one side there is a list of names of all the
heads-of-household in the town. Three adjacent columns of
figures (no names) are headed "Wife," "Children," and "Servants." In all, 421 persons are included in the census, and they are
distributed through 70 families.

These figures suggest a rough average of six persons per family
in the Bristol population of 1689. Closer examination shows that
households of four, five, and six persons were most common, comprising some 47 per cent of the whole sample; 17 per cent were
smaller than this (one to three people each), and 36 per cent were
larger.[7] These results may seem surprisingly low, in the light of
traditional notions about the size of the colonial family, but Bristol
was not an unusual community. As I have tried to show elsewhere
in greater detail,[8] the families of this town may have been slightly

5. *Mayflower Descendant,* VIII, 85.
6. Unfortunately, little is known about the origin of the census—by whom
it was compiled, and for what purpose. It survives thanks to a copy made
by George T. Paine of Providence, Rhode Island, and published in the *New
England Historical and Genealogical Register,* XXXIV (1880), 404–5. It
has been republished in Richard LeBaron Bowen, *Early Rehoboth* (Rehoboth, Mass., 1945), I, 75–76.
7. See Appendix, Table VI.
8. See John Demos, "Families in Colonial Bristol, Rhode Island: An Exercise
in Historical Demography," *Willam and Mary Quarterly,* 3d Ser., XXV
(1968), 40–57. A brief description of the early history of Bristol is in order,
since a good deal of the "quantitative" data presented hereafter comes from
this one census. The town was taken from the Indians as a result of King
Philip's War, and regular settlement began around the year 1680. Most of

larger than the norm for some other parts of the colony. But if so, the discrepancy was extremely narrow, and for our purposes the Bristol materials should be regarded as typical.

The simple categories of "husband," "wife," "children," and "servants" are probably as accurate and useful as any more modern terms we might contrive for describing the colonial family. In fact, only the last one requires some explication in order to be intelligible today; the other three can be directly transposed. These continuities of language obviously say a good deal about the essential similarity of the structure of families then and now. But even so, it will be worthwhile to stop and consider each one of the categories separately. For while basic meanings may have remained the same, we must recognize certain changes through time in the environmental circumstances which surround family life.

Mortality is perhaps the most powerful of these circumstances, and unfortunately there are as yet few sound investigations of its exact dimensions in the colonial period. There are plenty of florid images floating about—images of marriage regularly cut short by death, and whole families of children wiped out by disease—but all this is quite unfounded. Indeed the Plymouth Colony records suggest a standard of life and health that would compare favorably

the settlers came from adjacent Old Colony towns, such as Rehoboth and Swansea. They were a relatively young group and were presumably eager for the opportunities available to them in a new community. Bristol possesses a fine natural harbor, and in the eighteenth century it was to become a seaport of some consequence. However, in these early years it seems to have functioned chiefly as an agricultural town; the land was parceled out with this in mind, and only a few of the first generation of townsmen were active in trade. There are, in sum, three ways in which Bristol may have differed from other Plymouth Colony towns in 1689: the recency of its settlement, the relative youthfulness of its population, and its potentiality for a more commercial orientation. However, none of these factors is likely to have created serious distortions for our purposes: in terms of household size and structure Bristol may be regarded as a representative case. (For one modest exception to this statement, see below, p. 79.) For a more detailed account of the town's history see George L. Howe, Mount Hope: A New England Chronicle (New York, 1959), and George H. Munro, The History of Bristol, R.I. (Providence, 1880).

with that of any preindustrial society today. My own work with these materials is not conclusive, but it does at least offer some working hypotheses. Three of them can be briefly stated: (1) A man reaching adulthood (defined for the moment as the age of twenty-one) could expect to live to about seventy. For a woman the average was some seven years less. (2) The lower figure for women does, of course, reflect the hazards inherent in bearing children. Yet this factor can easily be exaggerated. It seems that a bit less than 20 per cent of the deaths among adult women were owing to causes connected with childbirth. Or, to put it another way, something like one birth in thirty resulted in the death of the mother. (3) The rate of mortality among infants and small children was also much lower than we have traditionally supposed. This is a difficult matter to study systematically because some deaths among the very young were not recorded in the usual fashion. However, the evidence that does exist suggests a maximum of 25 per cent mortality for the entire age span between birth and maturity (age twenty-one), and the real figure may well have been substantially less.[9] Of course, in our own day the comparable rate would be close to 1 per cent—so there certainly *are* real differences here. Still, the point remains that death was not the "usual circumstance," even in these remote and essentially primitive colonial settlements. It was, to be sure, an ever-present possibility, and few people can have gotten very far along in life without losing someone in their immediate circle of friends and relations. But in terms of the overall stability of family life it was not a factor of the first importance.

Death made its greatest impact when it struck at married adults, for the loss of one spouse obviously caused considerable dislocation within an individual family. Yet the problem was usually of limited duration, for many widows and widowers remarried

9. These conclusions are the outcome of considerable work with the vital records of the Old Colony. See Appendix, Tables II and III. For another, slightly more detailed statement, see John Demos, "Notes on Life in Plymouth Colony," *William and Mary Quarterly*, 3d. Ser., XXII (1965), 271.

within a relatively short space of time. Often the interval was less than a year, and in a few cases less than six months. We should not imagine here any lack of love for the departed spouse. It was rather a matter of custom, and indeed of sheer functional necessity. The man who lived out of the marital relation was rather awkwardly placed in terms of the larger community; moreover, he needed a wife's help in trying to maintain an efficient household. The same pressures worked with even greater force in the case of a widowed woman.

So it was that most families, within a given community at a given point in time, exemplified the basic model of husband, wife, and children. The situation in Bristol in 1689 can be precisely determined from the town census. Among the 70 families resident there, only two were headed by a single adult (one widow, and one widower). The remaining 68 were fully "intact," at least at this (adult) level.

It may also be useful to calculate the portion of people who actually lived out this sequence of marriage, bereavement, and remarriage. It was, in fact, considerable, but nothing that even approached a majority of the community as a whole. My investigation of some 700 people who lived to be at least fifty years old has shown the following: Among the men some 60 per cent were married just once; for the women the comparable figure was 75 per cent. Moreover, most of the remainder were people with two marriages; only 6 per cent of the men and 1 per cent of the women were married *more* than twice.[10] Thus the old stereotype of the doughty settler going through a long series of spouses one after the other needs to be quietly set aside.

So much (temporarily) for husbands and wives; let us turn now to the category of children. What was the extent of *their* membership in the households of the Old Colony? Once again the Bristol census offers the most powerful single piece of evidence. It reveals, first of all, that a majority of the total population of the

10. See Appendix, Table V.

town comprised children; the exact figure was 54 per cent. It also shows that the average number of children per family was slightly more than three, but that sets of one, two, three, four, and five were all common to a more or less equal degree. Above five children the sample tails off quite steeply. One-sixth of the families fall into this group (that is, over five children), and the largest single set is ten.[11] These results may seem a bit on the low side at first glance, but they must be viewed in context. It is important to remember that families grew rather slowly, and that the number of children in any particular household was a direct function of the age of the parents. There were certain very firm regularities in the spacing of births in the families of the colonists. The first child usually came along within fifteen months of the date of the marriage ceremony, often within twelve months—and occasionally, alas, within nine. (Of this, more later.) [12] Thereafter the normal spacing was about two years, though there was some tendency toward slightly longer intervals as the wife-and-mother grew older.

Note that young couples recently married were bound to contribute to the lower segment of any town sample, such as the one for Bristol. It was only as the parents neared middle age that their households might begin to show a really large number of children. But after middle age the process would reverse itself once again, since some of the older children would be leaving home to set up on their own. Thus there is nothing untoward about finding, simultaneously: (1) an average of three children per family for an entire community at any given point in time; and (2) a much higher average for children born to a particular couple during the whole span of their married lives. In actual fact, an examination of some 100 Old Colony couples for whom there is good information demonstrates that eight to nine children apiece was pretty standard.[13] Here, then, is one traditional belief about colonial

11. See Appendix, Table VII.
12. See below, pp. 158–59.
13. See Appendix, Table I.

family life which survives the test of the evidence—the notion, in short, that families reared extremely large numbers of children, at least by contrast to the norms of our own day.

There is one final point to mention with respect to the membership of children in these seventeenth-century households. Since births were usually spaced at intervals of two years or more, and since the whole period of childbearing for a given couple might encompass as much as twenty years, the children of each family comprised a community of persons of quite different ages and radically different stages of development. For example, the household of a man forty-five years old might well contain a full-grown son about to marry and begin his own farm, and an infant still at the breast, not to mention all of the children in-between. This is, of course, much in contrast to the situation that commonly prevails today, when parents not only have many fewer children alltold but also try to have them within a certain limited space of time. (The age at which the average American mother now has her last child is twenty-six.) The modern pattern tends to highlight the distance between the generations, and to make of childhood a quite tangible, or at least visible, condition. But in Plymouth Colony, and indeed in any society where the same sort of family predominates, these differences were considerably blurred. The way to maturity appeared not as a cliff to be mounted in a series of sudden and precarious leaps, but as a gradual ascent the stages of which were quite literally embodied in the many siblings variously situated along the way.

The category of "servants" presents the major obstacle to a clear understanding of the membership of colonial families. The term itself was used in a very general and imprecise way, and covered many situations which we must try at least briefly to differentiate. First, and most easily recognized in the light of our own meanings today, there was the hired man or woman. This was a grown person, who contracted to work in some family for a specified period of time (anywhere from several months to several years). Such arrangements show up in the Colony Records under the following format: "Thomas Bunting . . . put himself as a servant to dwell with John Cooke, Junir, . . . during the terme of eight yeares." [14] This was, of course, the "indentured servitude" long familiar to historians of the seventeenth century.

In some cases men and women were obliged to become servants as an act of discipline initiated by the community at large. Petty criminals and idlers were often handled in this way. Thus, for example, in 1644 the General Court found James Till guilty of committing a theft and ordered him to serve in the household of Timothy Hatherly for two years; his earnings were to be used to pay off his fine.[15] Some years later a certain "Goodwife Thomas, the Welchwoman" was directed to work and live with the family of Robert Barker—he also to have control over the management of her estate and "to see that shee doe not live extravigantly as formerly." [16] Obviously in these special cases the wishes of the individuals involved were not considered, but in most other respects the arrangement resembled the standard model of servitude.

Occasionally men would "put" themselves in other households in order to learn a particular craft or skill. Thus in 1667 "Richard Handy, . . . woolcomber, hath covenanted, agreed, and put himselfe an apprentice to and with James Skiffe, Junir, . . . cooper, to live with the said James from the 25th of October next en-

14. *Records of the Colony of New Plymouth, in New England*, ed. Nathaniel B. Shurtleff and David Pulsifer (Boston, 1855–61), II, 78. See also, *Plymouth Colony Records*, I, 8, for a similar, though short-term (seven months') agreement between Richard Church and William Barker. And also, *ibid.*, 92, 100, 103, 104.

15. *Plymouth Colony Records*, II, 69.

16. *Plymouth Colony Records*, III 197. In 1633 the Court placed Thomas Higgens, "having lived an extravigant life," with John Jenney for a term of eight years. *Plymouth Colony Records*, I, 21. And five years later Web Adey was presented for "disorderly liveinge in idlenesse & nastynes," set in the stocks, and directed to find himself a master. If he failed to do so, the Court would find him one. The order also made Adey arrange to rent or sell his house and garden in order to buy clothes "fitt for service." *Ibid.*, 87.

sueing untill that hee judge in himselfe that hee hath fully attained the skill and craft of a cooper." [17] Usually, however, the terms were less formal and specific than this. It must be said that the sum total of adult servants of all kinds, noted in some way in the Colony Records, was not large. Apparently much the greatest portion of persons in servitude were children, and to this group we must now give particular consideration.

The practice of "putting out" children touched a variety of different circumstances, only some of which can be reconstructed now. In certain instances the learning of a trade was central, and the terms of the contract defined a formal apprenticeship.[18] We know, moreover, that a master would ignore such terms only at his peril. In 1654 Jonathan Briggs, "sometimes servant to William Hailstone, of Taunton, complained agains his said mr that hee hath not pformed his covenants to him in that hee did not learn him the trad of a tayler." [19] The General Court ruled for the plaintiff and directed Hailstone to pay £ 15 in damages. Conversely, in another Court case a servant formally released his master from an obligation to "learne mee . . . the trade of a cooper," since "it hath bine onely by my neglect the above said ingagement hath not yett bine pformed." [20]

Yet in fact the actual records of this kind of specific training relationship are quite sparse; indeed the word "apprentice" was used as loosely as—and interchangably with—the vague term "servant." Most often the educational aspects of a contract were stated in quite general language. When John Phillips placed his son William in the household of John Bradford "after the manner of an Apprentice," Bradford agreed simply "to teach and instruct the

---

17. *Plymouth Colony Records*, IV, 194.
18. See, for example, the agreement whereby Samuel Jenney was bound to Kenelm Winslow "in the joyners occupacon." *Plymouth Colony Records*, I, 24.
19. *Plymouth Colony Records*, III, 51.
20. *Plymouth Colony Records*, VI, 31.

said apprentice, to write and read and give him that education as becometh a master to a servant." [21] Meanwhile Benjamin Savory went through two different "apprenticeships." In the first he was supposed to learn "whatsoever trad [his master] . . . can Doe"; [22] in the second he was to be instructed "in learning that is to say to read and write" and also "in husbandry." [23]

Still, we should not take lightly the clauses in these contracts which defined the obligation to teach at least two of the "three R's." For literacy was not widespread in this culture, and the ability to read and write must have been quite highly valued. Moreover, there was little formal schooling anywhere in the Old Colony until the last quarter of the century,[24] and the practice of placing children out may have constituted a functional equivalent for at least some of its young people. Perhaps, then, servants and apprentices were frequently the children of illiterate parents, moving into households which maintained a higher standard of education. But unfortunately these are very difficult relationships to prove.

It is easier, though, to analyze the standing of the different families involved, in terms of material wealth. And clearly, in certain cases, servants were leaving relatively poor families and going to wealthier ones. The indenture of Zachariah Eddy, for example, made all of this quite explicit. Eddy was only seven years old at the time, but his parents declared that they were obliged to put him out since they had "many children, & by reason of many wants lying upon them, so as they are not able to bring them up as they desire." The boy went into the household of Mr. John Browne of Rehoboth, "one of ye Assistants of this goument." Browne for his part promised to "bring him up in his imploymt of husbandry, or any busines he shall see meete for ye good of theire

21. This deed, from the Marshfield Town Records, is published in L. S. Richards, *History of Marshfield* (Plymouth, 1901), I, 28.
22. *Mayflower Descendant*, V, 91.
23. *Mayflower Descendant*, XII, 133.
24. See below, pp. 143–44.

child." [25] Yet there were also cases in which economic differentials could not have been an important factor. George Soule of Duxbury sent one of his daughters into the family of John Winslow—and *both* men were relatively well-to-do. Samuel Fuller's unusually complex household contained at the time of his death several servants of one type or another; but meanwhile his own daughter was living with "goodwife Wallen."

Still another factor behind many of these arrangements for putting children out was the death of one or both of the natural parents. In short, this was the way that seventeenth-century communities took care of orphans. Widow Mary Ring who died in 1631 left her young son Andrew to grow up in the family of her son-in-law Stephen Deane—requiring Deane "to help him forward in the knowledge & feare of God, not to oppresse him by any burthens but to tender him as he will answere to God." [26] Usually, when it was the husband who died first, the children were left in the day-to-day care of their mother. But if the widow remarried all of this might have to be changed. Some wills specifically anticipated this possibility: Anthony Besse's, for example, directed that, if his wife married again, "the five biggest [children] . . . bee put forth and theire Cattle with them according to the Descretion of the overseers." [27] In a few instances children were dispersed even though the widow lived on and did not remarry. Thus William Savill's will left only one of his three youngest children in the care of his wife; the other two were to be sent elsewhere. [28]

It must be confessed that when all of these reasons for transferring children from one household to another have been carefully laid out, there still remain some cases covered by none of them. That is, some of the children directly involved came from families that were very much intact, were relatively well-off, and had no lack of educational attainments; moreover, the contractual

25. *Plymouth Colony Records*, II, 112–13.
26. *Mayflower Descendant*, I, 30–31.
27. *Mayflower Decendant*, XIV, 152.
28. *Mayflower Descendant*, VII, 41–43.

arrangements made no mention whatsoever of learning a particular trade. The possibility arises, therefore, that some broader
social or personal values may have played into this whole pattern.
Edmund Morgan has suggested that parents in this culture "did
not trust themselves with their own children . . . [and] were
afraid of spoiling them by too great affection" [29]—hence the impulse to send them away into other homes. Unhappily there is no
way to confirm this with hard evidence. But among all the various
speculations that might be offered here, Morgan's still seems the
best one.

We should also like to know how common this practice was,
how many children were directly affected. The impression
created by reading dozens of wills and indenture contracts may
well be misleading, for the question must really be posed in terms
of some proportion of entire communities. Here again there is
only one piece of evidence that directly fronts the issue, namely,
the Bristol census for 1689. But if this is a representative source, it
suggests that the number of children living in households other
than those of their natural parents may not have been so great, at
least at any single point in time. In the census, the "servants" category comprises some 56 persons, or 13 per cent of the total population of the town. More than two-thirds of all the families listed
reported no servants at all; and only two showed a really large
complement (eight and eleven respectively.)[30] Most important of
all, there were four times as many "children" as "servants" reported in the whole census; and we should remember that the latter group must have included at least some adults who had hired
themselves out. In short, the great majority of Bristol's young people were apparently living in the homes of their own parents in
1689—perhaps as many as 90 per cent of them.

Still, the same pattern should ideally be assessed *through* time as
well, so as to reveal the proportion of children who spent *some*

29. Edmund Morgan, *The Puritan Family* (New York, 1966), 77.
30. See Appendix, Table VIII.

part of their early years living outside of the parental roof. This measure would serve to modify the picture somewhat, and might well take in as many as one-third of all the children. But without a sequence of several census reports there is no way to contrive an exact figure.

Hopefully it is now established that one married couple plus children and (in some cases) servants formed the model household unit in Plymouth Colony. But certain occasional variants on this pattern must be recognized at least briefly.

Most important was the residence in some households of aged grandparents. The community seems to have expected that old people no longer able to fend for themselves would find comfort and care in the families of their grown children. Husbands writing wills were particularly anxious to pin down these arrangements for the widows they would leave behind. William Carpenter of Rehoboth, for example, left his house to his son Samuel, with the stipulation that his widow "is to have the Rome I now lodge in and the Chamber over it and to have liberties to Come to the fier to Doe her occasions." [31] Thomas King's will provided much more detail: not only would his widow have "the East End of my dwelling house . . . with a liberty to make some use of the Cellars and and [sic] leantoos;" she would also receive "five pounds by the year paid to her and the one half of it in money the other half of it in Corne and other Provision also wood provided for her fire and winter meat and Sumer meat for two Cows." [32] Sometimes bequests to the children were made directly contigent on their performance of these filial duties. Josiah Winslow left all his movable properties to his wife, to be distributed at her death "to my Children accordingly as shee shall see cause and they Deserve, in thire Carryage and Care of her in her widdowes estate." [33] On

31. *Mayflower Descendant*, XIV, 232.
32. *Mayflower Descendant*, XXXI, 100–101.
33. *Mayflower Descendant*, XXXIV, 34.

other occasions when the dead man had failed to leave any will, his children might voluntarily agree to provide for their mother—witness the settlement of the estate of Thomas Crowell of Yarmouth, whereby his two sons "volluntory freely and willingly Condescended to maintaine our mother Agness Crowel . . . according to our abillities." [34]

There is also evidence that some men made arrangements of this kind even before their death—"retiring," in effect, on the "social security" provided by a willing child. The Colony Records contain a declaration by Lieut. Samuel Nash of Duxbury, who "being aged, and not in a capassety to live and keep house of himselfe, hath therefore put his estate into the hands of William Clarke, of Duxburrow, that thereby hee may have a comfortable lively-hood." Clarke, let it be noted, was married to Nash's daughter.[35] But occasionally these agreements were effected by men not formally related to one another. A pair of deeds from Marshfield in 1685 shows William White bestowing a large piece of land on John Branch, his "tenant," in exchange for £ 50 and a pledge that Branch "shall . . . hereafter Maintaine me the said William White Providing for & allowing unto me Convenient & sutable Meat Drinke apparil washing & lodging both in Sickness & in health dureing the terme of my naturall life." [36] Sometimes a will offers a retrospective look at the same pattern. Thus Andrew Ring made a special bequest to a certain one of his sons named William "seeing his son William Ring had for divers yeares past taken the

34. *Mayflower Descendant*, XI, 26.
35. *Plymouth Colony Records*, VI, 125–26. Not all of these "retirement" arrangements necessarily created joint households. In 1661, for example, Francis Sprague of Duxbury deeded his entire farm to his son John—on one condition. John was not to "enter upon the possession of house or land; till after the Decease of his father ffrancis Sprague but shall keep the house tenantable for his father During his fathers life." The son apparently would continue to live in another house of his own—exchanging a regular pattern of helpfulness for the promise of full ownership later on. See *Mayflower Descendant*, XVI, 206.
36. *Pilgrim Notes and Queries*, V, 88.

care of the family & bin the support of his old age & of his wife late deceased." [37]

The details of these arrangements often differed, but the outcome was presumably the same in all cases: the membership in some households of one or two older persons in addition to the central married pair. Another kind of variant showed the need in a few instances to find a place for unmarried adults, nearly always women. When a man died, leaving one or more daughters as yet unwed, he usually made special provision for them in his will. Stephen Hopkins, for example, left most of his estate to his son Caleb; but he also stipulated that his four daughters, who ranged in age from about fourteen to twenty-two "shall have free recourse to my house in Plymouth upon any occasion there to abide and remayne for such tyme as any of them shall thinke meet and conveyent & they single persons." [38] These situations rarely lasted for any great length of time, for most girls were married before they got very far into their twenties. Near the end of the century, however, spinsters became somewhat more common, as demographic trends worked to create a surplus of females in certain of the older towns of the Colony.[39] And these spinsters could only have lived in the households of some relative, normally a parent or brother.

A young man, by contrast, was never subject to living arrangements of this type. For when he attained his majority he would normally move out from under the parental roof—either to marry and begin his own family, or else to "be for himself" while remaining single for a while longer.[40] It is important to stress both of these alternatives, since it is not widely recognized that single

37. *Mayflower Descendant*, IV, 196.
38. *Mayflower Descendant*, XIII, 14.
39. For a somewhat larger discussion of this point see Demos, "Families in Colonial Bristol, Rhode Island: An Exercise in Historical Demography," 50–51.
40. See, for example, certain clauses in the will of John Churchill, Sr., in *Mayflower Descendant*, XVIII, 40–41.

men could, and sometimes did, live in households of their own. Until 1669 [41] Plymouth had no laws comparable to those in the Massachusetts Bay Colony which compelled unmarried persons to live under regular "family government." It does seem that proper form required single men to obtain town permission before starting their own separate homes. Thus, for instance, Plymouth in 1639 allowed John Carew "to be for himself upon the continuance of the good report of his carriage & demeanr . . . Edmund Weston is lycenced to live wth John Carew, & to be ptner with him in workeing and planting." [42] Conversely, the authorities might act to break up an establishment of this type which did not conform to accepted standards of decent behavior. A Court Order of 1653 directed that "teag Jones, and Richard Berry, and others with them bee caused to part theire uncivell living together." [43]

Indeed, one senses that a degree of suspicion attached to households composed of unmarried men; but the point remains that for many years no actual statutes opposed the practice. It is clear, finally, that such households did exist and function—with or without the permission of local officials. Their significance is implicit in orders like the following one, issued by a Marshfield town meeting in 1653: "It is agreed upon that all young men who are in the township that are single persons, and are at their own hands, shall be liable to pay all the town's rates as the rest of the inhabitants do, after the value of ten pounds a head for every such person." [44]

Old people, spinsters, single men: here, then, are three social categories which were bound to create some modification of the

41. In that year the following order was placed on the books: "Whereas great inconvenience hath arisen by single psons in this Collonie being for themselves and not betakeing themselves to live in well govrned families It is enacted by the Court that henceforth noe single pson be suffered to live of himselfe or in any Family but such as the Celectmen of the Towne shall approve of." William Brigham, *The Compact with the Charter and Laws of the Colony of New Plymouth* (Boston, 1836), 156.
42. *Plymouth Colony Records*, I, 135–36.
43. *Plymouth Colony Records*, III, 37.
44. Richards, *History of Marshfield*, I, 30.

basic nuclear family unit as previously described. But what can we say of the total importance of these alternative patterns? As usual, it is easy enough to illustrate that each alternative existed, but very hard to know what proportion of households were actually affected. Once again, the Bristol census is our only resource, and in this particular connection its utility is extremely limited. The census shows just one unmarried man living in a house of his own, though it does also record in a very ambiguous way two other persons who may fall into the same category. It provides no evidence whatsoever for the residence of elderly people or spinsters in the homes of relatives. At first sight this seems an astonishingly meager result—so much so, indeed, that one begins immediately to cast about for some explanation in terms of the particular demographic configuration of Bristol at the time. Happily, there *are* certain facts which come close to meeting these specifications. Bristol was still a relatively new town in 1689, and as I have tried to show elsewhere in some detail, its citizenry was quite youthful overall.[45] Most of the settlers had been in their twenties or early thirties when they first came there, and were just a few years older at the time the census was taken. Elderly people and "old maid" sisters did not, presumably, wish to move to an entirely new community. We know from the wills and land deeds that such people did form a part of *some* Old Colony households—but mostly, it seems, in the older and more established settlements. In a broad sense, then, the average household may well have been more clearly nuclear in "new towns" than in those which dated from the earliest period.

There is one last category of people to be considered here—a category of "unfortunates" who needed placement in some particular households for their own care and protection. They never formed a large group numerically, but they do serve to point up

45. This paragraph represents just a summary of certain matters discussed in more detail in Demos, "Families in Colonial Bristol, Rhode Island: An Exercise in Historical Demography," 44, 49–50.

rather vividly the wide range of functions which the family in this era was expected to serve. Here, for example, was an obvious way to handle some of the community's poorest citizens, people who simply could not make a living for and by themselves. A complicated set of Court deliberations in 1680–81 revolved around the case of John Harmon, a pauper who had been staying for some time with Robert Ransom of Plymouth. Harmon had lived previously in both Taunton and Plymouth, and there was some doubt as to which town should be responsible for the cost of his care (estimated by Ransom at three shillings per week).[46]

Harmon was not only poor—he was also "decriped," and it may be that most people in similar situations were suffering from a real physical disability. For, in a broad sense the treatment of serious illness was tied closely to the household setting. Of course, in the usual case a sick person would simply remain in his own home, under the watchful care of parents, spouse, or children. But occasionally illness came to someone who had no near relatives to look after him. Such a person would have to go to some other household, at least temporarily, and the town would pay for the arrangement.[47]

Moreover, certain men in the Colony acquired over time a reputation for medical knowledge, and probably took "patients" into their homes with some regularity. In the Marshfield records there is the notation (dated 1646) that "Josias Winslow and John Din-

46. *Plymouth Colony Records*, VI, 54, 74. It would be wrong, however, to suggest that this was the only, or even the major, way in which the settlers sought to provide for their poor. The more usual procedure was to encourage a poor man to keep his household together (assuming he had one to begin with), and to give him periodically some form of outside relief. Most towns, for example, seem to have maintained a common stock of cattle, which were farmed out to various poor families. Each family would have the milk from such cattle for its own use, and some portion of "the increase" (that is, calves born in the meantime). Occasionally, too, these procedures were supplemented by the direct allocation of money. For examples of all this in the town of Plymouth, see *Records of the Town of Plymouth* (Plymouth, 1889), I, 3–4, 8–9, 12, 20, 27, 29.
47. *Records of the Town of Plymouth*, I, 172.

gley were appointed by the town to take order that Roger Cooke be forthwith sent to Mr. Chauncey to cure, and for what they shall be at, either sending of him or in his cure, or for his diet and lodging, the town promist to save the said Josias and John Dingley harmless." [48] Roger Cooke was presumably a man without a family, and without the means to arrange for his own treatment. So the town stepped in, assumed financial responsibility, and sent Cooke to stay with Charles Chauncey of Scituate (whose talents as a physician were widely recognized).

It is, in sum, the combination of these two institutions—the family working *for* the town at large—that we must particularly notice. For in an era when there were no hospitals, no poorhouses, indeed no specialized welfare institutions of any kind, the *social* importance of the family was extremely large.

48. Richards, *History of Marshfield*, I, 27. A Court order of March 2, 1647 recognized Mr. Chauncey as an "approved phisition."

CHAPTER FIVE

HUSBANDS AND WIVES

❧

No aspect of the Puritan household was more vital than the relationship of husband and wife. But the study of this relationship raises at once certain larger questions of sex differentiation: What were the relative positions of men and women in Plymouth Colony? What attributes, and what overall valuation, were thought appropriate to each sex?

We know in a general way that male dominance was an accepted principle all over the Western World in the seventeenth century. The fundamental Puritan sentiment on this matter was expressed by Milton in a famous line in *Paradise Lost:* "he for God only, she for God in him;" and there is no reason to suspect that the people of Plymouth would have put it any differently. The world of public affairs was nowhere open to women—in Plymouth only males were eligible to become "freemen." Within the family the husband was always regarded as the "head"—and the Old Colony provided no exceptions to this pattern. Moreover, the culture at large maintained a deep and primitive kind of suspicion of women, solely on account of their sex. Some basic taint of corruption was thought to be inherent in the feminine constitution—a belief rationalized, of course, by the story of Eve's initial treachery in the Garden of Eden. It was no coincidence that in both the Old and the New World witches were mostly women. Only two allegations of witchcraft turn up in the official records of Plymouth,[1] but other bits of evidence point in the same general direction. There are, for example, the quoted words of a mother beginning an emotional plea to her son: "if you would beleive a woman beleive mee. . . ."[2] And why *not* believe a woman?

The views of the Pilgrim pastor John Robinson are also interesting in this connection. He opposed, in the first place, any tendency to regard women as "necessary evils" and greatly regretted the currency of such opinions among "not only heathen poets . . . but also wanton Christians." The Lord had created both man and woman of an equal perfection, and "neither is she, since the creation more degenerated than he from the primitive goodness."[3] Still, in marriage some principles of authority were essential, since "differences will arise and be seen, and so the one must give way, and apply unto the other; this, God and nature layeth upon the woman, rather than upon the man." Hence the proper attitude of a wife towards her husband was "a reverend subjection."[4]

However, in a later discussion of the same matter Robinson developed a more complex line of argument which stressed certain

1. The first occurred in 1661, in Marshfield. A girl named Dinah Silvester accused the wife of William Holmes of being a witch, and of going about in the shape of a bear in order to do mischief. The upshot, however, was a suit for defamation against Dinah. The Court convicted her and obliged her to make a public apology to Goodwife Holmes. *Plymouth Colony Records*, III, 205, 207, 211. The second case (at Scituate, in 1677) resulted in the formal indictment of one Mary Ingham—who, it was said, had bewitched a girl named Mehitable Woodworth. But after suitable deliberations, the jury decided on an acquittal. *Plymouth Colony Records*, V, 223–24.
2. From a series of depositions bearing on the estate of Samuel Ryder, published in *Mayflower Descendant*, XI, 52. The case is discussed in greater detail below, pp. 165–66.
3. *The Works of John Robinson*, ed. Robert Ashton (Boston, 1851), I, 236.
4. *Ibid*, 239–40.

attributes of inferiority assumed to be inherently feminine. Women, he wrote, were under two different kinds of subjection. The first was framed "in innocency" and implied no "grief" or "wrong" whatsoever. It reflected simply the woman's character as "the weaker vessel"—weaker, most obviously, with respect to intelligence or "understanding." For this was a gift "which God hath . . . afforded [the man], and means of obtaining it, above the woman, that he might guide and go before her." [5] Robinson also recognized that some men abused their position of authority and oppressed their wives most unfairly. But *even so*—and this was his central point—resistance was not admissible. Here he affirmed the second kind of subjection laid upon woman, a subjection undeniably "grievous" but justified by her "being first in transgression." In this way—by invoking the specter of Eve corrupting Adam in paradise—Robinson arrived in the end at a position which closely approximated the popular assumption of woman's basic moral weakness.

Yet within this general framework of masculine superiority there were a number of rather contrary indications. They seem especially evident in certain areas of the law. Richard B. Morris has written a most interesting essay on this matter, arguing the improved legal status of colonial women by comparison to what still obtained in the mother country.[6] Many of his conclusions seem to make a good fit with conditions in Plymouth Colony. The baseline here is the common law tradition of England, which at this time accorded to women only the most marginal sort of recognition. The married woman, indeed, was largely subsumed under the legal personality of her husband; she was virtually without rights to own property, make contracts, or sue for damages on her own account. But in the New World this situation was perceptibly altered.

5. *Ibid.*, 240.
6. Richard B. Morris, *Studies in the History of American Law* (New York, 1930), Chapter III, "Women's Rights in Early American Law."

Consider, for example, the evidence bearing on the property rights of Plymouth Colony wives. The law explicitly recognized their part in the accumulation of a family's estate, by the procedures it established for the treatment of widows. It was a basic principle of inheritance in this period—on both sides of the Atlantic—that a widow should have the use or profits of one-third of the land owned by her husband at the time of his death and full title to one-third of his movable property. But at least in Plymouth, and perhaps in other colonies as well, this expressed more than the widow's need for an adequate living allowance. For the laws also prescribed that "if any man do make an irrational and unrighteous Will, whereby he deprives his Wife of her reasonable allowance for her subsistencey," the Court may "relieve her out of the estate, notwithstanding by Will it were otherwise disposed; especially in such case where the Wife brought with her good part of the Estate in Marriage, or hath by her diligence and industry done her part in the getting of the Estate, and was otherwise well deserving." [7] Occasionally the Court saw fit to alter the terms of a will on this account. In 1663, for example, it awarded to widow Naomi Silvester a larger share of her late husband's estate than the "inconsiderable pte" he had left her, since she had been "a frugall and laborious woman in the procuring of the said estate." [8] In short, the widow's customary "thirds" was not a mere dole; it was her *due*.

But there is more still. In seventeenth-century England women were denied the right to make contracts, save in certain very exceptional instances. In Plymouth Colony, by contrast, one finds the Court sustaining certain kinds of contracts involving women on a fairly regular basis. The most common case of this type was the agreement of a widow and a new husband, made *before* marriage, about the future disposition of their respective properties.

7. Brigham, *The Compact with the Charter and Laws of the Colony of New Plymouth*, 281.
8. *Plymouth Colony Records*, IV, 46.

The contract drawn up by John Phillips of Marshfield and widow Faith Doty of Plymouth in 1667 was fairly standard. It stipulated that "the said Faith Dotey is to enjoy all her house and land, goods and cattles, that shee is now possessed of, to her owne proper use, to dispose of them att her owne free will from time to time, and att any time, as shee shall see cause." Moreover this principle of separate control extended beyond the realm of personal property. Phillips and widow Doty each had young children by their previous marriages, and their agreement was "that the children of both the said pties shall remaine att the free and proper and onely dispose of theire owne naturall parents, as they shall see good to dispose of them."[9] Any woman entering marriage on terms such as these would seem virtually an equal partner, at least from a legal standpoint. Much rarer, but no less significant, were contracts made by women *after* marriage. When Dorothy Clarke wished to be free of her husband Nathaniel in 1686, the Court refused a divorce but allowed a separation. Their estate was then carefully divided up by contract to which the wife was formally a party.[10] Once again, no clear precedents for this procedure can be found in contemporary English law.

The specific terms of some wills also help to confirm the rights of women to a limited kind of ownership even within marriage. No husband ever included his wife's clothing, for example, among the property to be disposed of after his death. And consider, on the other side, a will like that of Mistress Sarah Jenny, drawn up at Plymouth in 1655. Her husband had died just a few months earlier, and she wished simply to "Despose of som smale thinges that

9. *Ibid.*, 163–64. For another agreement of this type, see *Mayflower Descendant*, XVII, 49 (the marriage contract of Ephraim Morton and Mistress Mary Harlow). The same procedures can be viewed, retrospectively, in the wills of men who had been married to women previously widowed. Thus when Thomas Boardman of Yarmouth died in 1689 the following notation was placed near the end of his will: "the estate of my wife brought me upon marriage be at her dispose and not to be Invintoried with my estate." *Mayflower Descendant*, X, 102. See also the will of Dolar Davis, *Mayflower Descendant*, XXIV, 73.

10. *Mayflower Descendant*, VI, 191–92.

is my owne proper goods leaveing my husbands will to take place according to the true Intent and meaning thereof." [11] The "smale thinges" included not only her wardrobe, but also a bed, some books, a mare, some cattle and sheep. Unfortunately, married women did not usually leave wills of their own (unless they had been previously widowed); and it is necessary to infer that in most cases there was some sort of informal arrangement for the transfer of their personal possessions. One final indication of these same patterns comes from wills which made bequests to a husband and wife separately. Thus, for example, Richard Sealis of Scituate conferred most of his personal possessions on the families of two married daughters, carefully specifying which items should go to the daughters themselves and which to their husbands.[12] Thomas Rickard, also of Scituate, had no family of his own and chose therefore to distribute his property among a variety of friends. Once again spouses were treated separately: "I give unto Thomas Pincin my bedd and Rugg one paire of sheets and pilloty . . . I give and bequeath unto Joane the wife of the aforsaid Thomas Pincin my bason and fouer sheets . . . I give and bequeath unto Joane Stanlacke my Chest . . . unto Richard Stanlacke my Chest . . . unto Richard Stanlacke my best briches and Dublit and ould Coate." [13]

The questions of property rights and of the overall distribution of authority within a marriage do not necessarily coincide; and modern sociologists interested in the latter subject usually emphasize the process of decision-making.[14] Of course, their use of live samples gives them a very great advantage; they can ask their informants, through questionnaires or interviews, which spouse decides where to go on vacation, what kind of car to buy, how to discipline the children, when to have company in, and so forth.

11. *Mayflower Descendant*, VIII, 171.
12. *Mayflower Descendant*, XIII, 94–96.
13. *Mayflower Descendant*, IX, 155.
14. See, for example, Robert O. Blood, Jr., and Donald M. Wolfe, *Husbands and Wives* (Glencoe, Ill., 1960), esp. ch. 2.

The historian simply cannot draw out this kind of detail, nor can he contrive any substantial equivalent. But he is able sometimes to make a beginning in this direction; for example, the records of Plymouth do throw light on two sorts of family decisions of the very greatest importance. One of these involves the transfer of land, and illustrates further the whole trend toward an expansion of the rights of married women to hold property. The point finds tangible expression in a law passed by the General Court in 1646: "It is enacted &c. That the Assistants or any of them shall have full power to take the acknowledgment of a bargaine and sale of houses and lands . . . And that the wyfe hereafter come in & consent and acknowledg the sale also; but that all bargaines and sales of houses and lands made before this day to remayne firm to the buyer notwithstanding the wife did not acknowledge the same." [15] The words "come in" merit special attention: the authorities wished to confront the wife personally (and even, perhaps, privately?) in order to minimize the possibility that her husband might exert undue pressure in securing her agreement to a sale.

The second area of decision-making in which both spouses shared an important *joint* responsibility was the "putting out" of children into foster families. For this there was no statute prescribing a set line of procedure, but the various written documents from specific cases make the point clearly enough. Thus in 1660 "An Agreement appointed to bee Recorded" affirmed that "Richard Berry of Yarmouth with his wifes Concent and other frinds; hath given unto Gorge Crispe of Eastham and his; wife theire son Samuell Berry; to bee att the ordering and Disposing of the said Gorge and his wife as if hee were theire owne Child." [16] The practice of formally declaring the wife's consent is evident in all

15. Brigham, *The Compact with the Charter and Laws of the Colony of New Plymouth*, 86.
16. *Mayflower Descendant*, XV, 34.

such instances, when both parents were living. Another piece of
legal evidence describes an actual deathbed scene in which the
same issue had to be faced. It is the testimony of a mother confirming the adoption of her son, and it is worth quoting in some
detail. "These prsents Witnesse that the 20th of march 1657–8
Judith the wife of William Peaks acknowlidged that her former
husband Lawrance Lichfeild lying on his Death bedd sent for
John Allin and Ann his wife and Desired to give and bequeath
unto them his youngest son Josias Lichfeild if they would accept
of him and take him as theire Child; then they Desired to know
how long they should have him and the said Lawrance said for
ever; but the mother of the child was not willing then; but in a
short time after willingly Concented to her husbands will in the
thinge." [17] That the wife finally agreed is less important here than
the way in which her initial reluctance sufficed to block the
child's adoption, in spite of the clear wishes of her husband.

Another reflection of this pattern of mutual responsibility appears in certain types of business activity—for instance, the management of inns and taverns ("ordinaries" in the language of the
day). All such establishments were licensed by the General Court;
hence their history can be followed, to a limited degree, in the official Colony Records. It is interesting to learn that one man's license was revoked because he had recently "buryed his wife, and
in that respect not being soe capeable of keeping a publicke
house." [18] In other cases the evidence is less explicit but still revealing. For many years James Cole ran the principal ordinary in
the town of Plymouth, and from time to time the Court found it
necessary to censure and punish certain violations of proper deco-
rum that occurred there. In some of these cases Cole's wife Mary
was directly implicated. In March 1669 a substantial fine was imposed "for that the said Mary Cole suffered divers psons after

17. *Mayflower Descendant*, XII, 134.
18. *Plymouth Colony Records*, IV, 54.

named to stay drinking on the Lords day . . . in the time of publicke worshipp." [19] Indeed the role of women in all aspects of this episode is striking, since two of the four drinking customers, the "divers psons after named," turned out to be female. Perhaps, then, women had considerable freedom to move on roughly the same terms with men even into some of the darker byways of Old Colony life.

The Court occasionally granted liquor licenses directly to women. Husbands were not mentioned, though it is of course possible that all of the women involved were widows. In some cases the terms of these permits suggest retail houses rather than regular inns or taverns. Thus in 1663 "Mistris Lydia Garrett" of Scituate was licensed to "sell liquors, alwaies provided . . . that shee sell none but to house keepers, and not lesse than a gallon att a time;" [20] and the agreement with another Scituate lady, Margaret Muffee, twenty years later, was quite similar.[21] But meanwhile in Middlebury one "Mistress Mary Combe" seems to have operated an ordinary of the standard type.[22] Can we proceed from these specific data on liquor licensing to some more general conclusion about the participation of women in the whole field of economic production and exchange? Unfortunately there is little additional hard evidence on one side or the other. The Court Records do not often mention other types of business activity, with the single exception of milling; and no woman was ever named in connection with this particular enterprise. A few more wills could be cited—for instance, the one made by Elizabeth Poole, a wealthy spinster in Taunton, leaving "my pte in the Iron workes" to a favorite nephew.[23] But this does not add up to very much. The economy of Plymouth was, after all, essentially simple—indeed "underdeveloped"—in most important respects. Farming claimed

19. *Plymouth Colony Records*, V, 15.
20. *Plymouth Colony Records*, IV, 44.
21. *Plymouth Colony Records*, VI, 187.
22. *Ibid.*, 141.
23. *Mayflower Descendant*, XIV, 26.

the energies of all but a tiny portion of the populace; there was relatively little opportunity for anyone, man *or* woman, to develop a more commercial orientation. It is known that in the next century women played quite a significant role in the business life of many parts of New England,[24] and one can view this pattern as simply the full development of possibilities that were latent even among the first generations of settlers. But there is no way to fashion an extended chain of proof.

Much of what has been said so far belongs to the general category of the rights and privileges of the respective partners to a marriage. But what of their duties, their basic responsibilities to one another? Here, surely, is another area of major importance in any assessment of the character of married life. The writings of John Robinson help us to make a start with these questions, and especially to recover the framework of ideals within which most couples of Plymouth Colony must have tried to hammer out a meaningful day-to-day relationship. We have noted already that Robinson prescribed "subjection" as the basic duty of a wife to her husband. No woman deserved praise, "how well endowed soever otherwise, except she frame, and compose herself, what may be, unto her husband, in conformity of manners." [25] From the man, by contrast, two things were particularly required: "love . . . and wisdom." His love for his wife must be "like Christ's to his church: holy for quality, and great for quantity," and it must stand firm even where "her failings and faults be great." His wisdom was essential to the role of family "head"; without it neither spouse was likely to find the way to true piety, and eventually to salvation.

It is a long descent from the spiritual counsel of John Robinson to the details of domestic conflict as noted in the Colony Records. But the Records are really the only available source of information about the workings of actual marriages in this period. They

24. Elizabeth Anthony Dexter, *Colonial Women of Affairs* (Boston, 1911).
25. *The Works of John Robinson*, I, 20.

are, to be sure, a negative type of source; that is, they reveal only those cases which seemed sufficiently deviant and sufficiently important to warrant the attention of the authorities. But it is possible by a kind of reverse inference to use them to reconstruct the norms which the community at large particularly wished to protect. This effort serves to isolate three basic obligations in which both husband and wife were thought to share.

There was, first and most simply, the obligation of regular and exclusive cohabitation. No married person was permitted to live apart from his spouse except in very unusual and temporary circumstances (as when a sailor was gone to sea). The Court stood ready as a last resort to force separated couples to come together again, though it was not often necessary to deal with the problem in such an official way. One of the few recorded cases of this type occurred in 1659. The defendant was a certain Goodwife Spring, married to a resident of Watertown in the Bay Colony and formerly the wife and widow of Thomas Hatch of Scituate. She had, it seems, returned to Scituate some three or four years earlier, and had been living "from her husband" ever since. The Court ordered that "shee either repaire to her husband with all convenient speed, . . . or . . . give a reason why shee doth not." [26] Exactly how this matter turned out cannot be determined, but it seems likely that the ultimate sanction was banishment from the Colony. The government of Massachusetts Bay is known to have imposed this penalty in a number of similar cases. None of the extant records describe such action being taken at Plymouth, but presumably the possibility was always there.

Moreover, the willful desertion of one spouse by the other over a period of several years was one of the few legitimate grounds for divorce. In 1670, for example, the Court granted the divorce plea of James Skiffe "haveing received sufficient testimony that the late wife of James Skiffe hath unlawfully forsaken her lawfull husband . . . and is gone to Roanoke, in or att Verginnia,

26. *Plymouth Colony Records*, III, 174.

and there hath taken another man for to be her husband." [27] Of course, bigamy was always sufficient reason in itself for terminating a marriage. Thus in 1680 Elizabeth Stevens obtained a divorce from her husband when it was proved that he had three other wives already, one each in Boston, Barbadoes, and a town in England not specified.[28]

But it was not enough that married persons should simply live together on a regular basis; their relationship must be relatively peaceful and harmonious. Once again the Court reserved the right to interfere in cases where the situation had become especially difficult. Occasionally both husband and wife were judged to be at fault, as when George and Anna Barlow were "severly reproved for theire most ungodly liveing in contension one with the other, and admonished to live otherwise." [29] But much more often one or the other was singled out for the Court's particular attention. One man was punished for "abusing his wife by kiking her of from a stoole into the fier," [30] and another for "drawing his wife in an uncivell manor on the snow." [31] A more serious case was that of John Dunham, convicted of "abusive carriage towards his wife in continuall tiranising over her, and in pticulare for his late abusive and uncivill carryage in endeavoring to beate her in a deboist manor." [32] The Court ordered a whipping as just punishment for these cruelties, but the sentence was then suspended at the request of Dunham's wife. Sometimes the situation was reversed and the woman was the guilty party. In 1655, for example, Joan Miller of Taunton was charged with "beating and reviling her husband, and egging her children to healp her, bidding them knock him in the head, and wishing his victuals might coak him." [33] A few years later the wife of Samuel Halloway (also of

27. *Plymouth Colony Records,* V, 33.
28. *Plymouth Colony Records,* VI, 44–45.
29. *Plymouth Colony Records,* IV, 10.
30. *Plymouth Colony Records,* V, 61.
31. *Plymouth Colony Records,* IV, 47.
32. *Ibid.,* 103–4.
33. *Plymouth Colony Records,* III, 75.

Taunton) was admonished for "carryage towards her husband
. . . soe turbulend and wild, both in words and actions, as hee
could not live with her but in danger of his life or limbs." [34]

It would serve no real purpose to cite more of these unhappy
episodes—and it might indeed create an erroneous impression that
marital conflict was particularly endemic among the people of the
Old Colony. But two general observations are in order. First, the
Court's chief aim in this type of case was to restore the couple in
question to something approaching tranquility. The assumption
was that a little force applied from the outside might be useful,
whether it came in the form of an "admonition" or in some kind
of actual punishment. Only once did the Court have to recognize
that the situation might be so bad as to make a final reconciliation
impossible. This happened in 1665 when John Williams, Jr., of
Scituate, was charged with a long series of "abusive and harsh carriages" toward his wife Elizabeth, "in speciall his sequestration of
himselfe from the marriage bed, and his accusation of her to bee a
whore, and that especially in reference unto a child lately borne of
his said wife by him denied to bee legittimate." [35] The case was
frequently before the Court during the next two years, and eventually all hope of a settlement was abandoned. When Williams
persisted in his "abuses," and when too he had "himself . . .
[declared] his insufficency for converse with weomen," [36] a
formal separation was allowed—though not a full divorce. In fact,
it may be that his impotence, not his habitual cruelty, was the
decisive factor in finally persuading the Court to go this far. For
in another case, some years later, a separation was granted on
the former grounds alone.[37]

The second noteworthy aspect of all these situations is the
equality they seem to imply between the sexes. In some societies
and indeed in many parts of Europe at this time, a wife was quite

34. *Plymouth Colony Records*, V, 29.
35. *Plymouth Colony Records*, IV, 93.
36. *Ibid.*, 125.
37. *Plymouth Colony Records*, VI, 191.

literally at the mercy of her husband—his prerogatives extended even to the random use of physical violence. But clearly this was not the situation at Plymouth. It is, for example, instructive to break down these charges of "abusive carriage" according to sex: one finds that wives were accused just about as often as husbands. Consider, too, those cases of conflict in which the chief parties were of opposite sex but not married to one another. Once again the women seem to have held their own. Thus we have, on the one side, Samuel Norman punished for "strikeing Lydia, the wife of Henery Taylor," [38] and John Dunham for "abusive speeches and carriages" [39] toward Sarah, wife of Benjamin Eaton; and, on the other side, the complaint of Abraham Jackson against "Rose, the wife of Thomas Morton, . . . that the said Rose, as hee came from worke, did abuse him by calling of him lying rascall and rogue." [40] In short, this does *not* seem to have been a society characterized by a really pervasive, and operational, norm of male dominance. There is no evidence at all of habitual patterns of deference in the relations between the sexes. John Robinson, and many others, too, may have assumed that woman was "the weaker vessel" and that "subjection" was her natural role. But as so often happens with respect to such matters, actual behavior was another story altogether.

The third of the major obligations incumbent on the married pair was a normal and exclusive sexual union. As previously indicated, impotence in the husband was one of the few circumstances that might warrant a divorce. The reasoning behind this is nowhere made explicit, but most likely it reflected the felt necessity that a marriage produce children. It is worth noting in this connection some of the words used in a divorce hearing of 1686 which centered on the issue of a man's impotence. He was, according to his wife, "always unable to perform the act of generation." [41] The

38. *Plymouth Colony Records*, V, 39.
39. *Ibid.*, 40.
40. *Plymouth Colony Records*, IV, 11.
41. *Plymouth Colony Records*, VI, 191.

latter phrase implies a particular view of the nature and significance of the sexual act, one which must have been widely held in this culture. Of course, there were other infertile marriages in the same period which held together. But perhaps the cause of the problem had to be obvious—as with impotence—for the people involved to consider divorce. Where the sexual function appeared normal in both spouses, there was always the hope that the Lord might one day grant the blessing of children. Doubtless for some couples this way of thinking meant year after year of deep personal disappointment.

The problem of adultery was more common—and, in a general sense, more troublesome. For adultery loomed as the most serious possible distortion of the whole sexual and reproductive side of marriage. John Robinson called it "that most foul and filthy sin, . . . the disease of marriage," and concluded that divorce was its necessary "medicine." [42] In fact, most of the divorces granted in the Old Colony stemmed from this one cause alone. But adultery was not only a strong *prima facie* reason for divorce; it was also an act that would bring heavy punishment to the guilty parties. The law decreed that "whosoever shall Commit Adultery with a Married Woman or one Betrothed to another Man, both of them shall be severely punished, by whipping two several times . . . and likewise to wear two Capital Letters A.D. cut out in cloth and sewed on their uppermost Garments . . . and if at any time they shall be found without the said Letters so worne . . . to be forthwith taken and publickly whipt, and so from time to time as often as they are found not to wear them." [43]

But quite apart from the severity of the prescribed punishments, this statute is interesting for its definition of adultery by reference to a married (or bethrothed) *woman*. Here, for the first time, we find some indication of difference in the conduct expected of men

42. *The Works of John Robinson*, I, 241.
43. Brigham, *The Compact with the Charter and Laws of the Colony of New Plymouth*, 245–46.

and women. The picture can be filled out somewhat by examining the specific cases of adultery prosecuted before the General Court down through the years. To be sure, the man involved in any given instance was judged together with the woman, and when convicted their punishments were the same. But there is another point to consider as well. All of the adulterous couples mentioned in the records can be classified in one of two categories: a married woman and a married man, or a married woman and a single man. There was, on the other hand, no case involving a married man and a single woman. This pattern seems to imply that the chief concern, the essential element of sin, was the woman's infidelity to her husband. A married man would be punished for his part in this aspect of the affair—rather than for any wrong done to his own wife.

However, this does not mean that a man's infidelities were wholly beyond reproach. The records, for example, include one divorce plea in which the wife adduced as her chief complaint "an act of uncleanes" by her husband with another woman.[44] There was no move to prosecute and punish the husband—apparently since the other woman was unmarried. But the divorce was granted, and the wife received a most favorable settlement. We can, then, conclude the following. The adultery of a wife was treated as both a violation of her marriage (hence grounds for divorce) *and* an offense against the community (hence cause for legal prosecution). But for comparable behavior by husbands only the former consideration applied. In this somewhat limited sense the people of Plymouth Colony do seem to have maintained a "double standard" of sexual morality.

Before concluding this discussion of married life in the Old Colony and moving on to other matters, one important area of omission should at least be noted. Very little has been said here of love, affection, understanding—a whole range of positive feelings and

44. *Plymouth Colony Records*, III, 221.

impulses—between husbands and wives. Indeed the need to rely so heavily on Court Records has tended to weight the balance quite conspicuously on the side of conflict and failure. The fact is that the sum total of actions of divorce, prosecutions for adultery, "admonitions" against habitual quarreling, does not seem terribly large. In order to make a proper assessment of their meaning several contingent factors must be recognized; the long span of time they cover, the steady growth of the Colony's population (to something like 10,000 by the end of the century),[45] the extensive jurisdiction of the Court over many areas of domestic life. Given this overall context, it is clear that the vast majority of Plymouth Colony families never once required the attention of the authorities. Elements of disharmony were, at the least, controlled and confined within certain limits.

But again, can the issue be approached in a more directly affirmative way? Just how, and how much, did feelings of warmth and love fit into the marriages of the Old Colony? Unfortunately our source materials have almost nothing to say in response to such questions. But this is only to be expected in the case of legal documents, physical remains, and so forth. The wills often refer to "my loveing wife"—but it would be foolish to read anything into such obvious set phrases. The records of Court cases are completely mute on this score. Other studies of "Puritan" ideals about marriage and the family have drawn heavily on literary materials—and this, of course, is the biggest gap in the sources that have come down from Plymouth Colony. Perhaps, though, a certain degree of extrapolation is permissible here; and if so, we must imagine that love was quite central to these marriages. If, as Morgan has shown, this was the case in Massachusetts Bay, surely it was also true for the people of Plymouth.[46]

45. There are three separate investigations dealing with this question: Bowen, *Early Rehoboth*, I, 15–24; Joseph B. Felt, "Population of Plymouth Colony," in American Statistical Association *Collections*, I, Pt. ii (Boston, 1845), 143–44; and Bradford, *Of Plymouth Plantation*, xi
46. See Edmund Morgan, *The Puritan Family* (New York, 1966), esp. 46 ff.

There are, finally, just a few scraps of concrete evidence on this point. As previously noted, John Robinson wrote lavishly about the importance of love to a marriage—though he associated it chiefly with the role of the husband. And the wills should be drawn in once again, especially those clauses in which a man left specific instructions regarding the care of his widow. Sometimes the curtain of legal terms and style seems to rise for a moment and behind it one glimpses a deep tenderness and concern. There is, for example, the will written by Walter Briggs in 1676. Briggs's instructions in this regard embraced all of the usual matters— rooms, bedding, cooking utensils, "lyberty to make use of ye two gardens." And he ended with a particular request that his executors "allow my said wife a gentle horse or mare to ride to meeting or any other occasion she may have, & that Jemy, ye neger, catch it for her." [47] Surely this kind of thoughtfulness reflected a larger instinct of love—one which, nourished in life, would not cease to be effective even in the face of death itself.

47. *Plymouth Colony Records*, VI, 134–35.

CHAPTER SIX

PARENTS AND CHILDREN

❧

Egalitarianism formed no part of seventeenth-century assumptions about the proper relationship of parents and children. But at Plymouth this relationship involved a set of *reciprocal* obligations.

From the standpoint of the child, the Biblical commandment to "Honor thy father and mother" was fundamental—and the force of law stood behind it. The relevant statute directed that "If any Childe or Children above sixteen years old, and of competent Understanding, shall Curse or Smite their Natural Father or Mother; he or they shall be put to Death, unless it can be sufficiently testified that the Parents have been very Unchristianly negligent in the Education of such Children, or so provoked them by extreme and cruel Correction, that they have been forced thereunto, to preserve themselves from Death or Maiming." A corollary order prescribed similar punishment for behavior that was simply "Stubborn or Rebellious"—or indeed, for any sort of habitual disobedience.[1]

1. Brigham, *The Compact with the Charter and Laws of the Colony of New Plymouth*, 245.

The rightful authority of the parents is clear enough here, but it should also be noted that this authority was limited in several ways. In the first place, a child less than sixteen years old was excluded from these prescriptions; he was not mature enough to be held finally responsible for his actions. Disobedience and disrespect on the part of younger children were surely punished, but on an informal basis and within the family itself. In such cases, presumably, the purpose of punishment was to form right habits; it was part of a whole pattern of learning. But for children of more than sixteen different assumptions applied.[2] Ultimate responsibility could now be imputed, and an offense against one's parents was also an offense against the basic values of the community. Hence the full retributive process of the laws might properly be invoked.

The clause relating to "extreme and cruel correction" implied a second limitation on parental power. The child did have the right to protect his own person from any action that threatened "Death or Maiming." Finally, it seems significant that the arbiter of *all* such questions was not the parental couple directly involved but rather the constituted authorities of the Colony as a whole. The correct response to gross disobedience in a child was as follows: "his Father and Mother, . . . [shall] lay hold on him, and bring him before the Magistrates assembled in Court, and testifie unto them, that their Son is Stubborn and Rebellious, and will not obey their voice and chastisement." [3] This may sound rather menacing, but it did imply an important kind of negative. The parents shall *not* take matters completely into their own hands. The child shall also have *his* say in Court; and presumably he may try, if he wishes, to show that his behavior was provoked by some cruelty on the part of his parents.

2. Sixteen was also the age at which children became fully liable in actions of lying and slander. See below, Chapter Ten, for a review of this and other evidence bearing on adolescence as a "developmental stage."
3. Brigham, *The Compact with the Charter and Laws of the Colony of New Plymouth*, 245.

It must be said that only a few cases of youthful disobedience to parents actually reached the Courts, and that these few are not very revealing. Certainly the death penalty was never invoked on such grounds; only once, in fact, was it even mentioned as a possibility. In 1679 "Edward Bumpus for stricking and abusing his parents, was whipt att the post; his punishment was alleviated in regard hee was crasey brained, otherwise hee had bine put to death or otherwise sharply punished." [4] In other instances the Court's function was to mediate between the affected parties or to ratify an agreement which had already been worked out on an informal basis. In 1669, for instance, it heard various testimonies about the "crewell, unnaturall, and extreame passionate carriages" of one Mary Morey toward her son Benjamin, and his own "unbeseeming" response. The situation was described as being so "turbulent . . . that severall of the naighbours feared murder would be in the issue of it." [5] Yet in the end the Court took no action beyond admonishing both principals and making them "promise reformation." Some years earlier Thomas Lumbert of Barnstable complained formally that "Jedediah, his sone, hath carryed stuburnly against his said father," and proposed that the boy be "freed, provided hee doe dispose himselfe in some honest family with his fathers consent." [6] The Court merely recorded this arrangement and decided not to interfere directly unless Jedediah neglected to find himself a good foster home. In sum, then, the role of the Court with regard to specific cases of this type, was quite limited. The laws on the matter should be viewed as expressing broad and basic values rather than an actual pattern of intervention in the day-to-day affairs of Old Colony households. In fact, most parents must have tried to define and enforce their authority very much on an individual basis. Quite likely an appeal to

4. *Plymouth Colony Records*, VI, 20.
5. *Plymouth Colony Records*, V, 16.
6. *Plymouth Colony Records*, III, 201.

the Courts was a last resort, to be undertaken only with a keen sense of failure and personal humiliation.

The innermost dimensions of these vital intrafamily relationships cannot really be traced. But two particular matters seem noteworthy. Questions of inheritance were more closely intertwined with discipline in that period than is generally the case now. In some of the wills bequests to certain children were made contigent on their maintaining the proper sort of obedience. Thus, for example, Thomas Hicks of Scituate left most of his lands to "my two sonnes Daniell and Samuell upon this proviso that they bee Obedient unto theire mother and carrye themselves as they ought soe as they may live comfortably together but if the one or both live otherwise then they ought and undewtyfully and unquietly with theire Mother . . . then hee that soe carryeth himselfe shall Disinheritt himselfe of his pte of this land." [7] The effectiveness of this kind of sanction among the settlers at large is difficult to assess. In many cases, of course, the point was never rendered so explicit as in the will of Thomas Hicks; but it must often have loomed in the background when conflict between parents and children reached a certain degree of intensity.

The same model of filial behavior seems to have obtained for grown as well as for young children, though perhaps in a somewhat attenuated form. In 1663, for example, the Court summoned Abraham Pierce, Jr. "to answere for his abusive speeches used to his father." [8] The younger Pierce was at this time twenty-five years old and married. Another Court case of a different sort involved a question of disputed paternity. Martha, wife of Thomas Hewitt, gave birth shortly—*too* shortly—after their marriage: her husband contended that he could not have been the child's father and so persuaded the Court. Instead suspicion pointed toward Martha's own father, Christopher Winter, raising thereby the

7. *Mayflower Descendant*, XI, 160.
8. *Plymouth Colony Records*, IV, 47.

awful specter of incest. Among the evidence presented was "Winters acknowlidgment, that after hee had had knowlidge of his said daughters being withchild,—being, as hee said, informed by Hewitt,—hee did not bring them together and enquire into it, nor reprove or beare witnes against her wickednes, as would have become a father that was innosent." [9] Apparently then, a parent would normally continue to concern himself directly in the personal affairs of his children, even when they had become adult and were involved with families of their own. And, by implication, the children should listen to his counsel and respond accordingly.[10]

But if the child owed his parents an unceasing kind of obedience and respect, there were other obligations which applied in the reverse direction. The parent for his part must accept responsibility for certain basic needs of his children—for their physical health and welfare, for their education (understood in the broadest sense), and for the property they would require in order one day to "be for themselves." There were, moreover, legal provisions permitting the community to intervene in the case of parents who defaulted on these obligations. One statute affirmed that when "psons in this Gourment are not able to provide Competent and convenient food and raiment for theire Children," the latter might be taken in hand by local officials and placed in foster families where they would be more "comfortably provided for." [11] Another, more extended set of enactments dealt with the whole educational side of the parental role. Children should be taught to read, "at least to be able duely to read the Scriptures." They should be made to understand "the Capital Laws" and "the main Grounds and Principles of Christian Religion." And they should be trained "in some honest lawful calling, labour or employment,

9. *Plymouth Colony Records*, V, 13.
10. On the question of property relationships between parents and grown children, see below, pp. 164–70.
11. *Plymouth Colony Records*, XI, 111.

that may be profitable for themselves, or the Country." [12] Parents
who neglected any of this were subject to fines; and once again
the ultimate recourse of transferring children into new families
might be applied if the neglect were habitual. Unfortunately we
cannot discover how often these procedures were actually set in
motion. The responsibility for specific cases was assigned to local
authorities in the various towns, and records of their actions have
not survived. But the basic intent behind the laws which covered
such matters is clear—and in itself significant.

The obligation to provide a "portion" of property for children
when they attained maturity was nowhere expressed in formal,
legal terms. But it can certainly be inferred from other types of
evidence. Many wills made specific mention of previous bequests
to grown children—real or personal property, or both. Deeds of
apprenticeship and adoption sometimes included the promise of a
portion as one of the essential terms. This responsibility might, it
seems, be transferred from a child's natural parents to his new
master, but it could not be overlooked altogether. Some men
gained the assistance of the government in arranging portions for
their young, witness the following type of Court Order: "Libertie
is graunted unto Mr. John Alden to looke out a portion of land
to accomodate his sons withall." [13] Indeed the fundamental laws of
the Colony recognized a special claim to such "accomodation" for
"such children as heere born and next unto them such as are heere
brought up under their parents and are come to the age of
discretion." [14]

More often, however, portions were managed on a purely private basis. One of the rare personal documents to survive from the
Old Colony, a letter written by Benjamin Brewster, describes the

12. Brigham, *The Compact with the Charter and Laws of the Colony of
New Plymouth*, 270-71.
13. *Plymouth Colony Records*, III, 120.
14. Brigham, *The Compact with the Charter and Laws of the Colony of
New Plymouth*, 46.

process as it operated in a particular case: "Being at the hose of Gorge Geres upon the first of may in the yere of our Lord: 1684 then and there was a discorse betwene the aforesayd Geres and his son Jonathan he then being of age to be for him selfe: upon som consederration mofeing the sayd Geres there to he then declared what he would gefe his son Jonathan as the full of his porshon except ypon his sons better behaver should desarve more which was: 130: akers of Land that his father had of Owanneco up in the contre: and: 2: best of 2 yere old: 1: stere of: 4: yer old and a cow." [15]

15. *Mayflower Descendant*, II, 113.

CHAPTER SEVEN

MASTERS AND SERVANTS

❧

We have already seen that the term "servant" conveyed a very broad meaning in the seventeenth century—that, indeed, it covered the whole spectrum of persons who might be resident in a given household but not a member of the immediate family. Still there were certain general conditions which obtained for virtually all servants, of whatever particular category.

In the first place and most simply, they were in the fullest sense integrated into the basic day-to-day functioning of the household. Every servant "lived in," as we would say today; moreover, his master assumed full responsibility for meeting all of his essential needs. The formal contracts between the parties concerned would usually specify these as "meate, drink and apparrell & lodging." [1] The Colony Records show that failure to fulfill these responsibilities might involve a master in legal proceedings. In 1657, for example, the Court investigated a complaint from a servant in Taunton

1. As, for example, in the contract binding Sarah Hoskins to Thomas and Winifred Whitney, in January 1644. See *Plymouth Colony Records*, II, 67–68.

"that hee is ill vsed, being decriped, and is in want of competent and convenient clothing." [2] Such cases were quite rare, however, and we may infer that the basic necessities were generally provided.

The duties of a master might also extend beyond the sphere of material wants, particularly in the case of *young* servants. As noted earlier, educational provisions were sometimes written into the indenture deeds; the master would promise at a minimum to teach his new charge to read and write. Moreover, there was a further responsibility for the spiritual development of the servant. Periodic urgings by the Colony government that the young be "catechized" and otherwise surrounded by religious influences were directed equally to parents and masters. In short, then, the prevalent assumptions about family life made little distinction between a natural child and a servant of about the same age. For most purposes, especially at the level of everyday care and supervision, the master would perform as a surrogate parent.

Of course, the adult servant, who hired him*self* out for a given period of time, was exempt from some aspects of this pattern. There is no evidence that such a person would expect to be taught anything in particular by his master—either a trade, or literacy, or Christian behavior. His compensations, besides board and room, were strictly financial; and in good times hired men might command six to ten pounds in wages per year.[3] Often even a younger servant might look forward to some special reward at the end of his term. Thus in 1679 a "covenent" between John Dingley and "Arthur Loe, his servant" promised a final payment of three

---

2. *Plymouth Colony Records*, III, 119. Note also this entry in the Records, some years earlier: "Jan. 20, 1632. Robt Barker, servt of John Thorp, complayned of his mr for want of clothes. The complaint being found to be just, it was ordered, that Thorp should either foorthwth apparrell him, or else make over his time to some other that was able to provide for him." *Ibid.*, I, 7.
3. See, for example, the agreements between Richard Bishop and Love Brewster (*Plymouth Colony Records*, I, 103), and Edward Shaw and Robert Bartlett (*ibid.*, 104).

This oil painting of Edward Winslow was done in London in 1651, probably by Robert Walker. It is the only known likeness of a member of the original Mayflower group. (Courtesy of Pilgrim Hall, Plymouth, Mass.)

The Harlow Old Fort House, Plymouth, Mass., view of the north and east sides. This house, built in 1677, is basically of single-bay, story-and-a-half design. However, there are rather large lean-to additions along the north and west sides. (Courtesy of the Plymouth Antiquarian Society. Photo credit, Robert I. Frank.)

The Harlow Old Fort House, Plymouth, Mass., view of the south and west sides. (Courtesy of the Plymouth Antiquarian Society. Photo credit, Robert I. Frank.)

The Major John Bradford House, Kingston, Mass., view of the front (south) side. This house, built by a grandson of Governor William Bradford, has two distinct parts. The western half (on the left in this photograph) was constructed in 1674, on the usual single-bay plan. In 1717 a large addition was made (right side of the photograph), comprising full-size rooms on both the first and second floors. Thus, as it appears today, the house is larger than the average Plymouth Colony dwelling. (Courtesy of the Bradford House Council, Kingston, Mass. Photo credit, Robert I. Frank.)

The Major John Bradford House, Kingston, Mass., view of the west side. (Courtesy of the Bradford House Council. Photo credit, Robert I. Frank.)

The hall fireplace and hearth, Harlow Old Fort House, Plymouth, Mass. (Courtesy of the Plymouth Antiquarian Society. Photo credit, Robert I. Frank.)

The kitchen fireplace and hearth, Major John Bradford House, Kingston, Mass. This is part of a lean-to addition at the rear (north side) of the house. (Courtesy of the Bradford House Council. Photo credit, Robert I. Frank.)

View of the hall, southwest corner, Major John Bradford House, Kingston, Mass. The furnishings are representative of the period, except for the rug at the lower left. (Courtesy of the Bradford House Council. Photo credit, Robert I. Frank.)

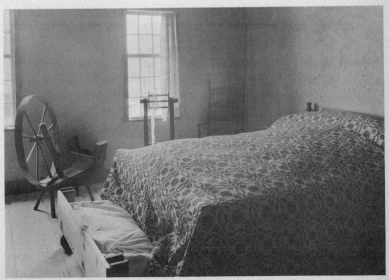

View of a second-floor "chamber," Harlow Old Fort House, Plymouth, Mass. Note the trundle bed. (Courtesy of the Plymouth Antiquarian Society. Photo credit, Robert I. Frank.)

A large 17th-century chest (wainscot type, one drawer), originally in the Morton family. (Courtesy of Pilgrim Hall, Plymouth, Mass.)

A trunk found at East Dennis, Mass. (formerly Plymouth Colony), original owner unknown. The lid bears the date 1687, and the initials W/A.E. (Courtesy of Pilgrim Hall, Plymouth, Mass.)

A collection of wooden tableware, originally in the John Alden house (no longer standing), Duxbury, Mass. (Courtesy of Pilgrim Hall, Plymouth, Mass.)

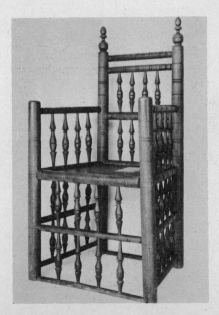

A chair, said to have been the property of Gov. William Bradford. This handsome object, made of pine and maple, was of course finer than the domestic furnishings found in most Old Colony households. (Courtesy of Pilgrim Hall, Plymouth, Mass.)

Letter of William Bradford (son of the Governor) to a brother, dated March 27, 1680. The letter refers briefly to arrangements for the marriage of Bradford's daughter. (Courtesy of Pilgrim Hall, Plymouth, Mass.)

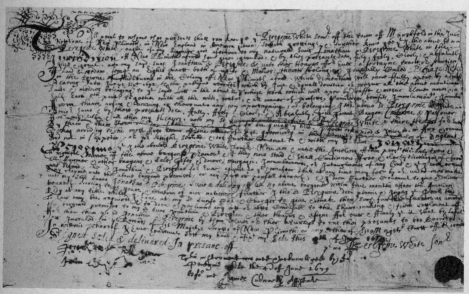

Deed, for gift of lands, from Peregrine White to his sons Jonathan and Peregrine, dated June 4, 1679. (Courtesy of Pilgrim Hall, Plymouth, Mass.)

pounds, "and incase hee carry well . . . four pounds."[4] In another instance some years earlier the agreement was for certain specified articles of clothing, a heifer, and twelve bushels of Indian corn.[5] Finally, too, there were those contracts which seem to have outlined a virtual adoption and in which the promise of a portion was implicit. Such, presumably, was the meaning of a central clause in the contract which placed young Samuel Berry in the service of George Crispe and his wife: The Crispes promised to "provide for the said Samuell in all thinges as theire owne Child; and afterwards if hee live to marry or to goe away from them; to Doe for him as if hee were theire owne Child."[6]

The master's basic responsibilities continued unaltered even if his servant experienced some serious—conceivably incapacitating—misfortune. Injury and illness were always real possibilities, of course, but this was the chance a master took. He was bound to protect his servant's welfare to the full extent of his ability, until the end of the contracted term; there was no shortening of this term except by mutual agreement.[7] An early Court case that revolved persistently around this issue included as principals Stephen Hopkins, one of the original Mayflower passengers, and a maidservant of his named Dorothy Temple. In 1639 Dorothy gave birth to an illegitimate child—fathered, it seems, by a convicted murderer named Peach, whom the Colony had recently executed. Hopkins was plainly incensed by this sequence of events, and he sought to turn both mother and infant out of his house for good. But the Court ruled otherwise. Its opinion stated "that in regard

4. *Plymouth Colony Records*, VI, 25.

5. The contract binding Samuel Eaton to John Cooke, *Plymouth Colony Records*, I, 43.

6. *Mayflower Descendant*, XI, 34. See also the contract binding Martha Everson to John Barrow, in *Records of the Town of Plymouth*, I, 112.

7. The law was quite explicit on this matter: "In case . . . any servant or servants . . . by Gods pvidence shall fall diseased lame or impotent by the way or after they come here, they shal be mayntayned and pvided for by their said masters etc during the terme of their services covenants, although their said masters release them out of their said service." *Plymouth Colony Records*, XI, 40.

by her covenant of indenture shee hath yet above two yeares to serve him, that the said mr Hopkins shall keepe her and her child, or pvide shee may be kept wth food and rayment during the said terme; and if he refuse so to doe, that then the collony pvide for her, and Mr Hopkins to pay it." [8] Sometime later, when it was evident that Hopkins would not comply with this order, the Court felt obliged to cite him for contempt. Eventually another resident of Plymouth agreed to take in the unfortunate pair; but Stephen Hopkins was forced to finance the new arrangement.[9]

We must recognize at least briefly certain exceptions to this general profile of life in servitude. For example, servants who differed racially from the colonists themselves were probably subjected to a rather special set of conditions. The records do not permit any detailed exploration of this matter, but the wills make one point abundantly clear: Negro and Indian servants were usually considered part of a dying man's estate, and were passed on to his heirs along with other sorts of "property." [10] The practice with a white servant, by contrast, was to bequeath the remainder of his contract—in short, a certain *period of time* in service, not the man himself.[11] Another type of exception was the really affluent household which counted a large number of servants among its members. In such households the servants may have formed a more separate group than was normally the case.

8. *Plymouth Colony Records*, I, 111.
9. *Ibid.*, 113.
10. The estate of John Dicksey of Swansea, who died in 1674, included "I Negro Mayde servant named Malle" valued at £24. *Mayflower Descendant*, XXV, 121. John Gorham's inventory (1675) listed "I Negro man" (no value given). *Mayflower Descendant*, IV, 156. Anthony Snow of Marshfield directed in his will (1692) that "my Indian maid servant" pass to his wife (among other bequests). *Mayflower Descendant*, V, 2. The inventory of Capt. Thomas Willet of Marshfield (taken in 1674) included "8 Negroes" valued at £200. *Mayflower Descendant*, XXXIII, 35.
11. The inventory of the estate of Joseph Halway of Sandwich (made in 1647) noted the following: "Ther is two years and an half servis in a boy but hee is a very bad servant." *Mayflower Descendant*, VIII, 209. Samuel Wilbore of Taunton left to "son Shadrack the time of the service of my man John Mockelett a Scotsman." *Mayflower Descendant*, XIV, 151.

We cannot definitely prove this, but it appears to make sense from a purely logistical standpoint. There is also an interesting and relevant detail from testimony given during an inquest into the death of a laborer named Henry Drayton in 1655. He was last seen alive in the house of Mr. Edward Winslow of Marshfield, where he had—so it was reported to the Court—"suped with the servants." [12] Winslow was one of the wealthiest men in the Colony, and the evidence that his servants "suped" apart from the family proper seems to imply a significant principle of differentiation within the household. Perhaps, indeed, the internal arrangements of establishments like this one harked back to the medieval manor house, with its large membership and variety of status definitions.

However, the actual number of servants embraced by these atypical situations cannot have been large. Negro and Indian servants were very uncommon at Plymouth until after the Old Colony period; and few householders were anywhere near as well off as Winslow. The Bristol census for 1689 puts both cases into proper perspective. It shows only two families with more than three servants. And among the whole servant population of the town it mentions just one Negro.

Surely, then, most servants lived on quite intimate terms with the families of their masters; but intimacy did not in this case imply equality. The fundamental posture of the servant should be "respect and obedience," and he was, in theory, always at his master's beck and call. In particular, he must "not absent himselfe from . . . service by night or day, without [the master's] consent." [13] Servitude on these terms was a twenty-four-hour proposition.

The Colony Records suggest, however, that actual performance often fell considerably short of these requirements. In his own

12. *Plymouth Colony Records*, III, 70.
13. From the contract between Arthur Loe (servant) and John Dingley (master), in *Plymouth Colony Records*, VI, 25.

study Edmund Morgan has pointed to the labor shortage that plagued New England throughout the seventeenth century.[14] This condition, he argues, gave to servants a definite advantage in establishing the actual day-to-day substance of a working relationship with their masters, and helped to render chronic a certain degree of servant misbehavior. Plymouth appears to provide a good case in point. The Court Records show many hearings in which the issue was some act of truancy, or disobedience, or theft, on the part of a servant. A few of them can be sampled here. In 1644 Charles Thurstone, servant to Mr. William Hanbury, was convicted of "abuseing his mris" and sentenced to be whipped; he was, however, then released after making a promise of good behavior for the future, thanks in part to "a petition exhibited by the yeong men of Plym." [15] Two years later he was again before the Court for "his . . . misdemeanor, and revelling, & disguised daunceing." [16] In 1660 Philip Pointing, hired man in the household of Henry Hobson, was arraigned on such grounds as these: (1) "hee being sent for a caske of liquor, drew out and desposed amongst his consorts two quarts and upwards, and put water in the caske"; (2) "defaming . . . [his master] . . . in saying hee was a theife and had stollen hogges and steer." [17] In 1658 John Barnes asked the Court simply to void his contract with a servant named Wade, saying that the latter "ran up and downe like unto a runagate, and hee could have no comaund over him." [18]

Unscheduled and unapproved absences formed one of the most troublesome of all the areas of misconduct by servants, and the Court stood ready to take whatever action might seem appropriate in any specific case. Some habitual runaways were ordered whipped; and some were directed simply to make up the time that

14. Morgan, *The Puritan Family*, 125 ff.
15. *Plymouth Colony Records*, II, 73.
16. *Ibid.*, 105.
17. *Plymouth Colony Records*, III, 18:
18. *Ibid.*, 126.

had been lost to their masters.[19] Occasionally the court also indicted other members of the community who had encouraged a servant in his delinquency. Thus, for example, when a dispute between Thomas Dexter Jr. and his servant Robert Ransom came to trial in 1654, a third party drew a fine "for entertaining him, the said Ransome, into his house, and otherwise indescretly carrying towards him wherby hee was abetted in his stubburnes against his said master." [20] Some cases of this type simply reflected the anguish of a young child forced to live apart from his natural parents. In 1643 the Court was forced to deal with Joseph Billington—age five—who "did oft depte his . . . masters service" in order to run home to his own family. The boy himself apparently seemed too young to punish, so the Court contrived other preventive measures. It decreed that "if either the said Francis, or Christian, his wyfe"—these were Joseph's parents—"do receive him, if he shall againe dept from his said master wthout his lycence, . . . the said Francis, and Christian, his wyfe, shalbe sett in the stocks . . . as often as he or shee shall so receive him." [21]

But the master's authority to control the life of his servant, while virtually total in some respects, was quite definitely limited in others. The right to dispose of a man's labor was not a license to exploit and abuse him in a personal sense. Many different types of restraint were effective in this connection. Some were essentially internal—religious principals of right conduct, fear of community disapproval—and are for this reason impossible to recover in any tangible form today.[22] But others were more formal and explicit.

19. See, for example, *Plymouth Colony Records*, II, 105.
20. *Plymouth Colony Records*, III, 64. See also *Plymouth Colony Records*, I, 46 (a certain "Whitney" convicted of "detayning another man's servt"); and *ibid.*, 118 (John Emerson "presented" and fined "for entertaineing of other mens servants at unlawfull tymes").
21. *Plymouth Colony Records*, II, 58–59.
22. Morgan has brought together some illuminating quotations from sermons and essays by Puritan clergymen in Massachusetts Bay, in connection with the religious sanctions against mistreatment of servants. See his *The Puritan Family*, 115 ff.

The Court, for example, was empowered to intervene directly in cases of gross mistreatment or negligence. The most gruesome episode of this kind came to light in 1655, in the course of an inquest into the death of John Walker, a thirteen-year-old servant to Robert Latham. When found, Walker's body was "blackish and blew . . . the skine broken in divers places, . . . all his backe [covered] with stripes given him by his master." [23] Further investigation disclosed a whole sequence of cruelties leading up to the final tragedy: frequent and unreasonable whippings, demands for heavy work far beyond a young boy's capacity, periodic deprivation of food and warm clothing. One affecting detail suggests the kind of anxiety which such treatment aroused in the boy himself: "hee . . . did constantly wett his bedd and his cloathes, lying in them, and soe suffered by it, his clothes being frozen about him." The master, Latham, was eventually tried and convicted of manslaughter, and sentenced to be "burned in the hand, . . . and . . . all his goods . . . confiscate." [24]

But clearly this case was in no sense representative; it may indeed have expressed a really special, and pathological, element of personal sadism. The more usual issue was some lesser degree of overwork, or physical abuse; and the outcome, typically, was a sharp "admonition" to the master involved. Occasionally, too, the Court would take steps to find the servant a new situation altogether.[25]

It is significant that a servant might sometimes act in his own

23. *Plymouth Colony Records*, III, 71.
24. *Ibid.*, 73.
25. See, for example, the hearing in 1640 which involved a "servant boy" named Roger Glass. Since his master John Crocker "is proved to have corrected [him] . . . in a most extreame & barbarous manner," the Court transferred his contract to another man. *Plymouth Colony Records*, I, 141. Servant girls were subject to one particular type of abuse which the Court was most anxious to prevent; namely, unwanted sexual advances by the master (or some member of his family). In 1655, for instance, Robert Peck of Rehoboth was fined "for laciviouse carriages and unchast in attempting the chastitie of his fathers maide servant, to satisfy his fleshly, beastly lust, and that many times for some yeares space." *Plymouth Colony Records*, III, 75.

behalf to lodge a complaint with the Court. This was true of several of the cases already cited.[26] In 1644 William Hatch and his servant "Hercules" came before the Court as equal parties in a dispute over the length of the latter's contract; and the decision went in favor of Hercules.[27] The interests of a younger servant in such matters might well be taken in hand by his own parents—if still living. Thus in 1655 John Hall of Yarmouth brought Francis Baker to Court for abusing his son Samuel "by kicking of him and otherwise unreasonably stricking of him." (Samuel had been bound to service in the Baker household.) Apparently the specific charge could not be substantiated, and the parties involved ended by arranging for the return of the boy to his own family. His father, however, made a payment of £8 to cover the remainder of his contracted time.[28]

Perhaps the most telling kind of evidence in this general connection comes from the wills and bears on the servitude of young persons whose parents had died. One concrete example should make the point sufficiently clear. The will of widow Ring, written in 1631, left careful instructions as to the future care of her youngest son Andrew. He was to go to live with his sister and brother-in-law (Elizabeth and Stephen Dean), but at the same time to be under the ultimate disposition of two older men, Samuel Fuller and Thomas Blossom, who were also the "overseers" of the Ring estate. His mother urged that he "have recourse unto these two my loving friends for councell & advice & to be ruled by them in anything they shall see good & convenient for him." Moreover, "if my Overseers shall see it meet to dispose of my

26. See, for example, the complaints brought by "a servant belonging to Mr. Thomas Gilbert Junir" (*Plymouth Colony Records*, III, 119), and by Robert Barker (*Plymouth Colony Records*, I, 7). Note, too, that in 1634 John Smith was able to take his master Edward Doty to Court in order to bring about an adjustment of his contract. It seems that Smith, "being in great extremity formerly," had bound himself to Doty for ten years; the Court now cut this term in half. *Ibid.*, 23.

27. *Plymouth Colony Records*, II, 69.

28. *Plymouth Colony Records*, III, 83, 88.

soone Andrew otherwise than with his Brother Deane That then my son Deane shall be willing to consent unto it, & they to dispose of him, provided it be alwaies wth the good will of my sonne Andrew." [29]

Here, then, is a pattern of divided control which one finds repeated in will after will. The child is placed with a foster family; and day-to-day supervision of his life falls to the head of that family, the man who becomes officially his "master." Yet *other* men are designated as his guardians in a broader sense: with them rests the power to effect long-term changes in his circumstances. Above all, they act as overall judges of his living situation—his whole relation to the master. They can, if they see fit, remove him from the one household and find him another, whether or not the first master approves.[30] Finally, in this as in most other wills, the boy's own wishes are explicitly taken into account. Thus there was relatively little likelihood that an orphaned child might be bound for any long period of time to an unsuitable or uncongenial family.

In working so closely with the legal evidence on servitude, and in emphasizing the matter of duties and restraints, we are in danger of losing sight of another, more informal side of the whole relationship—one that involved, above all, a broad range of positive ties and feelings. Kindness, loyalty, deep affection: surely such things formed a central part of many master-servant situations. This, at any rate, seems a logical deduction from the other, more directly accessible facts of the matter—from the youth of so many servants, from the long duration of their contracts, from the intimacy which characterized all their interactions with the master and his family. There is also the tangible evidence of the wills, the

29. *Mayflower Descendant,* I, 31.
30. The will of Alexander Winchester of Rehoboth, written in 1647, provides a further illustration of this pattern. His children, it seems, were already bound out into other families, but he directed that his overseers "have power upon complaint made by any of my children unto them to Remove them and thayer portions with them." *Mayflower Descendant,* IX, 30.

many instances in which a master left to his servant a generous gift of property. Thomas Morton of Plymouth bequeathed his entire estate "to my welbeloved friend and late faithfull Servant Samuel Gardiner of the Town . . . aforesaid who hath lived with me and whome I have brought up from his Childhoode . . . in Consideration of . . . love and Good affection." [31] The will was written in 1688 and Morton apparently had no direct heirs, no wife or children, living at the time. Gardiner, for his part, was then just over thirty years old, and had married and begun his own family some six years earlier.

If this represents a kind of extreme case, more modest gifts were fairly common. The will of William Palmer made bequests to all the surviving members of his family—and also one to "Moyses Rowly whom I love." [32] Rowly had been living in the Palmer household as a servant for several years. The Rev. Ralph Partridge of Duxbury left to "Joseph Prior my man servant my first Calfe of this yeare." [33] And Samuel Newman directed that a gift of ten shillings be made after his death to each of his "old servants Mary humpheres, of Dorchester; Elizabeth Cubby of Weymouth Elizabeth Palmer, of Rehoboth, and Lydia Winchester my present servant." [34] Especially striking in the Newman will is the geographical dispersion of the persons cited. In an era when distance created serious impediments to communication, it seems significant that a master should have asked his overseers to seek out and reward such a far-flung group of servants.

31. *Pilgrim Notes and Queries*, V, 122.
32. *Mayflower Descendant*, II, 148.
33. *Mayflower Descendant*, XIV, 229.
34. *Mayflower Descendant*, XV, 235.

CHAPTER EIGHT

WIDER KIN CONNECTIONS

The evidence that Plymouth households were basically nuclear in structure has been presented in an earlier chapter. It remains to add here a caution against making too much of this fact. We should not imagine that each family unit lived in isolation from all the others, including those to which it was related by blood. On the contrary, the sources from the period show a considerable degree of interconnection among kin.

There is, initially, the matter of physical contiguity—the possibility that neighbors, in the Old Colony towns, were often related as parents and children, or siblings, or cousins. This possibility would seem to pivot on certain questions of inheritance. One can imagine, for example, that a father might decide to break up his own estate in order to establish his children on adjoining subsections of it. Did this happen at Plymouth, and if so, how often? A final answer to such questions can only come from a comprehensive effort to map all the landholdings of all the settlers. Nothing on this scale has ever been attempted; so, for the present, tentative conclusions are all we can manage. It does seem clear, however, from the analysis of many individual deeds, that close relatives occasionally lived next to one another—but not really often.

The will of John Washburn of Bridgewater, who died in 1688, is revealing in this connection.[1] Most of Washburn's sons were by this time fully adult and had begun to farm lands of their own. It is obvious, however, from certain clauses in the will that the father had simply detached these lands from his own original holdings and given them to his sons as portions. Their proximity to one another is implicit in the description of their various boundaries. Thus at the time of his death John Washburn was living on land that was bordered on three sides by farms belonging to his sons. And the same pattern can be inferred for a number of other families as well.[2]

However, the opportunity to establish one's sons nearby was apparently a function of wealth. Washburn was among the most affluent residents of Bridgewater, and the same can be said of most similar cases. But the situation that prevailed in more "average" families was very nearly the reverse. The original holdings of most men simply were not large enough to accommodate the needs of grown children as well. At the same time many people did manage to acquire additional lands in some new township, or even in a frontier area, which made suitable portions for their young. George Soule, for example, left his main holdings in Duxbury to his eldest son John. But his will also mentions some earlier bequests of land—to two other sons in Dartmouth, and to two daughters in Middleborough.[3] Benjamin Bartlett left his home at Duxbury to one of his sons—and willed to three others various

1. *Mayflower Descendant*, XV, 248–51.
2. For example, the families of Henry Andrews of Taunton (whose will is in *Mayflower Descendant*, XI, 152–56); Richard Sears of Yarmouth (will in Samuel P. May, *The Descendants of Richard Sares [Sears] of Yarmouth, Mass.* [Albany, N.Y., 1890], 36–37); and John Gorham of Yarmouth (inventory of his estate and the settlement among his heirs in *Mayflower Descendant*, IV, 157 ff.)
3. *Mayflower Descendant*, II, 81–83.

properties in Middleborough, Little Compton, and Rochester.[4] Here, then, inheritance worked in the direction of scattering the younger generation, rather than holding it close to the parental hearth.

Of course, these cases are only one reflection of a much larger process of dispersion which spanned the entire length of the Old Colony period. Quite apart from specific bequests, there was always the obvious fact of empty land out beyond the line of settlement. Such land constituted a powerful lure for people of all kinds and classes. Quite often, one suspects, it induced younger men to turn away from a modest inheritance in the communities of their birth in order to embrace a wider field of opportunity elsewhere.

But there is other evidence which reflects in a more affirmative way on the importance of the bonds between kinfolk. The custom of "putting out" children, as servants and apprentices, merits some further consideration here. Scholars have not appreciated how frequently such arrangements followed the lines of family connection; yet for Plymouth the point seems indisputable. Sometimes careful genealogical checking is needed to bring out the fact, but in many other cases it is all quite explicit. We have, for instance, already examined the plan of the widow Ring to leave her son Andrew in the care of his much older sister and brother-in-law.[5] Just before his death Nathaniel Tilden made a similar arrangement for the two youngest of his own children.[6] His will directed that a grown son, Joseph, maintain them "for meate drink apparell & lodging"—although "my . . . wyfe shall have the education and Disposeing of them."

Often, too, such children were placed in the homes of uncles and aunts. When William Gilson of Scituate died in 1639, one of his chief heirs was a nephew named John Dammen—who "had beene a long tyme his servant and his kinsman too & he haveing no

4. *Mayflower Descendant*, VI, 44–46.
5. See above, p. 73.
6. *Mayflower Descendant*, III, 220.

child." [7] By way of contrast: Samuel Ryder of Plymouth wrote a will that purposely excluded his son Joseph from any inheritance because "he went wn young To his uncle who has done for him considerably." [8] In 1647 the Court recorded the fact that Richard Burt of Taunton "makes choyce of his uncle, James Burt, to be guardian unto him, & to live wth him during his minority." [9] (This is a rare case in which the functions of day-to-day and long-term supervision seem to have been joined in one "master.")

Grandparents were also directly involved in some of these situations. John Brown of Swansea wrote in his will: "Conserning all my five Children I Doe wholly leave them all to the ordering and Disposeing of my owne father . . . for him to bring them up not once questioning but that his love and Care for them wilbee as it hath bine for my selfe." [10] Brown's wife survived him, and the children probably remained under her immediate care; but ultimate responsibility for their welfare was clearly transferred to their grandfather. In 1679 the Court passed a special order granting to one John French a tract of land from the estate of his late grandfather. This action was taken "in reference unto severall yeers service pformed by John French unto John Kingsley, his grand father, in his life time." [11]

---

7. *Ibid.*, 160–62. Dammen apparently had some difficulty in establishing his right to all of the lands in question, for several years later the Court was obliged to take action to "clear up the aforsaid right". An important piece of testimony concerned the granting of the lands to Gilson in the first place and included the following: "whereas William Gillson . . . in his life time did require earnestly of the townsmen aforsaid severall pcells of land for accomodation of the sd William Gillson but being inquired of him by us whose names are heer underwritten the reason of his desire of so mutch land, being ancient & haveing no isew of his body to inherite the same after him, his answare was, yt hee had brought over with him into New England two of his sisters children from thaire parents, and was bound in conscience both to take care & to pvide for them as if thay weer his owne." *Plymouth Colony Records*, II, 142.
8. *Mayflower Descendant*, XI, 186.
9. *Plymouth Colony Records*, II, 119.
10. *Mayflower Descendant*, XVIII, 14–15.
11. *Plymouth Colony Records*, VI, 4. It is interesting that John Robinson in an essay entitled "Of Children and Their Education," strongly warned

Another case involved four orphaned children in Barnstable.[12] The circumstances, though unusually complicated, are worth unravelling in some detail for the light they throw on several different aspects of kinship connection. The children were born to Henry and Abigail (Bishop) Coggin during the 1640's. Their father died in about 1648, and their mother was soon remarried to another man, himself a widower, named John Finney. The children apparently followed her into Finney's own household. But five years later their mother too was dead, and John Finney was preparing to marry still another time. At this point he apparently wrote a letter to his late wife's father (and the children's grandfather), Thomas Bishop, who was then living in England. The letter asked for firm directions as to what should be done with the four young Coggins. Bishop's reply ordered the following. The only girl, Abigail, was "speedy to come home to mee for I purpose to take her as a Daughter." As for her brother Thomas: "I Doe Comite him to youer care and trust that you Doe provide for him and keep him as youer owne child taking his meanes to healp to his maintenance." Another boy named John should "bee bound in boston or Salem to that Trad his Genes Doe best lead him to but if it could bee to a Seaman that hee might come for England some time that I might see him or if you thinke good when I send for his sister to send him alsoe with her." The third boy, Henry, must remain with Finney "as youer oune sonne to Scoole and to write and Read till hee bee fitt for a Master." Thus two of the children continued to live in the Finney household, and two went elsewhere. But the striking thing is the way all this was decided. It was assumed that ultimate responsibility for the children's welfare belonged not to their step-

---

against permitting children to be brought up by their grandparents. The latter, he felt, "are more affectionate towards their children's children, than to their immediates" and this created very real danger of a "too great indulgence." *The Works of John Robinson*, I, 246.

12. *Mayflower Descendant*, VIII, 203–4.

father (who had known them on intimate terms for some five years) but to their grandfather (who probably had never seen them at all). This surely is a powerful comment on the importance which the colonists attached to ties of blood.

Some men left direct gifts to people outside the immediate circle of wife and children. The majority of such cases involved grandchildren. Henry Andrews of Taunton left to one grandson "a silver pint cupp with a silver cover to it," and to another a cow worth five pounds.[13] Robert Barker of Duxbury bequeathed substantial amounts of land to several grandchildren, whose father (Barker's son) had previously died.[14] Indeed this was Barker's main concern in writing his will; his gifts to other children and grandchildren were quite modest by comparison. William Thomas, a "gentleman" of Marshfield, left most of his property to his son Nathaniel, but also specified the way in which it would pass to certain grandchildren *after* the son's own death.[15]

The wills of people who had no direct descendants are especially relevant to an understanding of some of the wider ramifications of kinship. Almost invariably in such cases the chief beneficiaries were brothers and sisters, nephews and nieces. Thus the widow Ann Attwood, whose large estate has already been mentioned in another connection, made a certain nephew named William Crow her chief heir.[16] Token gifts to her brother and sister were justified on the ground that she and her late husband had "formerly showed [them] what healp and kindnes wee Could." John Wood of Middleborough died unmarried in 1673 and left to his mother "the rent of [his] ... house and land During her life." [17] After her death the estate was to pass to Wood's two

13. *Mayflower Descendant*, XI, 153. See also the will of Humphrey Turner (*Mayflower Descendant*, XXIV, 43) for several bequests to grandchildren; and that of Capt. Thomas Willett (*Mayflower Descendant*, XXVI, 80).
14. *Mayflower Descendant*, XXXI, 102.
15. *Mayflower Descendant*, X, 162–64.
16. *Mayflower Descendant*, XI, 200–201.
17. *Mayflower Descendant*, XXIV, 133.

youngest brothers and a sister. When John Curtice of Scituate died without leaving a will in 1680, the Court moved to settle his property among his four siblings.[18] Interestingly enough, the eldest surviving brother got a double share. The common practice of the Court in settling the estate of a man who died intestate was to give a double portion to his eldest son; and clearly its decision in the Curtice case mirrored this principle. John Hazell of Seekonk apparently had no close relatives of any kind when he wrote his will in 1651. But he inserted the following clause: "I give unto every one that Can make it appeare that they are my kindred twelve pence a peece if they shall Demaund the same." [19]

A few summary comments are needed to tie together the rather scattered materials of this little chapter. Direct bloodlines were accorded a special sort of precedence in the family feeling of the colonists: a man was involved, first of all, with his wife and children, and then with his grandchildren. Somewhat less intense was the relation to his own brothers and sisters, and to their children. Parent-child; grandparent-grandchild; brother (or sister)-brother (or sister); uncle (or aunt)-nephew (or niece): this was the general order of priority. But except for the will of John Hazell there is no evidence that notions of family and kin extended to a wider field of relationship. First cousins may have been recognized as such—but the fact implied no special feelings or responsibilities.

Yet within these rather narrow limits, ties of kinship did assume a considerable measure of importance. They were the determining factor in virtually all matters of inheritance. They helped, in at least a few instances, to shape residential patterns. And they provided the context for a great many of the arrangements whereby children were transferred from one household to another in the role of servants or apprentices. It is instructive to think of these patterns alongside the average situation in contemporary Amer-

18. *Plymouth Colony Records*, VI, 39.
19. *Mayflower Descendant*, X, 200.

ica; and in doing so what seems immediately striking is the high degree of overall similarity between the two periods. Our own sense of kinship conforms to just about the same set of boundaries. And, aside from the one important matter of child transfer, the activities and emotions which these boundaries normally enclose seem today little different from what obtained three centuries ago among the people of Plymouth Colony.

PART THREE

THEMES OF
INDIVIDUAL DEVELOPMENT

The various relationships discussed in the preceding chapters constituted significant elements in the actual ongoing lives of many individual persons. And it is important now to study these lives from another perspective—to try to see them more nearly as a whole, and to pay particular attention to their own continuities (or discontinuities) through time. This approach is what psychologists call the "developmental" one, and its result, ideally, is the portrayal of a complete "life-cycle."

There are, however, few good precedents for an effort to correlate historical facts with psychological theory, and part of what follows is plainly exploratory. Thus it may be wise to suggest at the outset some of the very real problems, and potential dividends, specific to this particular enterprise. The problems arise, in part, from the gaps in the available data—gaps of a sort that any historian can well imagine even in advance. They also reflect large areas of ambiguity and incompletion in developmental theory itself. There is, for example, a marked lopsidedness in most work on the life-cycle, a tendency to concentrate very heavily on the years before maturity. By contrast, the periods of middle and old age receive only passing attention. This distribution of emphasis can perhaps be explained in terms of the predominant influences on psychological study in recent decades; but it is hard to *justify*, from any larger standpoint.

There is, further, a fundamental problem of selection, since the historian finds not one, but several developmental theories at his disposal. How such choices are to be made, on what criteria, and to what ends: these questions belong to a different and much more "philosophical" book. But a personal statement of the choices made *here*, and elaborated in the next three chapters, does seem in order. My overall model of individual development is the one presented in the work of Erik Erikson—what he has called the "eight stages of man." This scheme tries to bring together important aspects of growth and conflict in the biological, the psychic, and the cultural settings. Each of the different stages relates to some particular issue, some fundamental "psycho-social" task and its resolution both in the individual person and in society as a whole. There is, of course, no need to hold rigidly to one theoretical scheme or style; a certain ecleticism may even be healthy in this type of work. Some of the questions raised by the Plymouth materials do seem to invite the use of alternative theories, Freudian, neo-Freudian, and non-Freudian. Still, every reader will recognize my larger order of preference, my strong conviction that Erikson has constructed the best working model of personality that we have, at least as yet.

One final problem worth mentioning is the possibility that the developmental sequence has itself been in motion—has altered in some ways over time. But Erikson's theory is in my view particularly receptive to this possibility, since it recognizes quite explicitly the importance of historical process. Indeed historians may well make a special contribution to the further progress of any such theory, for by testing it against the record of earlier periods and societies they may be able to show which of its parts are most unyielding, and which are most variable, in relation to particular cultural settings. To anticipate Chapter Ten for just a moment: it seems likely that adolescence, for example, was never before our own time an especially dramatic and difficult stage of life.

But with all these reasons for caution, we may still hope to derive important advantages from using a developmental perspective. Consider, as a general point, the study of children and their role in society at large. The relatively few historical works on this subject have for the most part applied static and undifferentiated views of childhood.[1] They have missed what I see as the really essential task—the need to discover the dynamic interconnections between experience at an earlier and a later stage, to appreciate that a child is always *developing*, according to influences that proceed from within as well as from the wider environment. It makes, in short, a very real difference that a particular event occurs earlier or later, that love or fright or encouragement or restriction enters the child's world at one time rather than another. His experience of "outside" pressures locks together with his own *internal* developmental necessities at any given moment, and the outcome may be of lasting consequence for his future.

In every case, therefore, it is necessary to ask not only how the culture has treated its constituent members but also how it has distinguished between different stages and periods of growth. There is neither the space—nor the data—to fashion a really full account of these matters in the pages that follow. But hopefully there is gain even in a rather fragmentary picture—one which serves at the very least to highlight some of the broad themes and fundamental turning points in any life shaped by the environment of seventeenth-century Plymouth.

1. See, for example, Sandford Fleming, *Children and Puritanism* (New Haven, Conn., 1933); and Alice Morse Earle, *Child Life in Colonial Days* (New York, 1927). The same sort of defect can, in my opinion, be attributed to more recent and more sophisticated studies, even to the superbly insightful study by Phillipe Aries, *Centuries of Childhood*, trans. Robert Baldick (New York, 1962).

CHAPTER NINE

INFANCY AND CHILDHOOD

❧

Surely no event in the life-cycle displays a greater difference between the conditions prevalent then and now than the first one—the crisis of birth itself. The usual setting, in its most general outlines, is easily imagined. Delivery would take place at home. Tradition has it that the "inner room" (see above, p. 31) in the familiar house plan was also known as the "borning room," in reference to its special use in times of childbirth. There the mother was brought to bed, and there presumably she remained until she and her infant child were strong enough to venture forth into the household at large. Her attendants were older women experienced in such matters and acting in the role of midwives.

In our own culture childbirth normally presents few difficulties of any magnitude; but in the seventeenth century it was quite another story. We have noted already the evidence that in one out of thirty deliveries the mother would lose her life,[1] or, stated another way, that every fifth woman in the Old Colony died from causes associated with childbirth. The mortality rate for newborn

1. See above, p. 66.

infants is more difficult to determine, but one in ten would seem a reasonable guess. These figures may seem surprisingly low when set alongside more traditional notions of life in the seventeenth century; but they nonetheless describe a very real danger. And this danger must have profoundly affected the perceptions of everyone directly involved in any given delivery.

When a baby was safely past the hazards of his first few days of life, he was doubtless incorporated quickly into the ongoing routine of his household. One major public event in which he took center stage was his baptism. Usually this occurred within six months of birth,[2] and on some occasions, particularly in wintertime, it must have been quite an ordeal. Otherwise, he enjoyed a continuing round of sleep and nourishment. The matter of how and where he slept is uncertain. Wooden and wicker cradles are among the most appealing artifacts of the seventeenth century to have come down to us today; but they are not found often in the inventory lists. Perhaps some of them were too crude and of too little value to bother with in adding up a man's estate. Perhaps, too, some other kind of makeshift bed was contrived for the newborn; or possibly he would for a short period sleep alongside his parents. It does seems that within a few months he was moved elsewhere—most likely to a trundle bed, which he might share with some of his older siblings. One rather gruesome notation in the Court Records serves to illustrate this type of arrangement. A small child of "about halfe a yeer old" had been "found dead in the morning...lying in bed with Waitstill Elmes and Sarah Hatch, the childs sister." An official board of inquest studied the matter and concluded that "either it was stiffled by lying on its face or accidentally over layed in the bed."[3]

The infant's clothing was probably quite simple. Previous stud-

2. Such at least is the impression one gains from examining the vital records of the Old Colony towns. In a considerable number of cases the records show both a date of birth and a date of baptism.
3. *Records of the Colony of New Plymouth, in New England,* ed. Nathaniel B. Shurtleff and David Pulsifer (Boston, 1855–61), VI, 45.

ies of this subject have turned up no evidence of swaddling or otherwise binding the child so as to restrict his movement.[4] Some type of linen smock seems to have been standard dress for seventeenth-century babies; and doubtless, too, they were frequently under several layers of woolen blankets.

The baby's nourishment consisted, it appears, entirely of breast milk. The subject is not much discussed in any documents extant today, but there are occasional, incidental references to it.[5] There is also the indirect evidence which derives from the study of birth intervals. We touched on this matter briefly in an earlier section, but it deserves a more extended statement here. In the average family, we noted, children were spaced roughly two years apart (or a bit longer near the end of the wife's childbearing span). This pattern is consistent with a practice of breast feeding a child for about twelve months, since lactation normally presents a biological impediment to a new conception.[6] The exceptions can nearly always be explained in the same terms. When one finds an interval of only twelve or fifteen months between two particular deliveries, one also finds that the older baby died at or soon after birth. (Here there would be no period of breast feeding, to speak of, and hence nothing to delay the start of another pregnancy.) [7]

4. My authority in this matter is Earle, *Child Life in Colonial Days*, 21 ff., 34 ff.
5. For example, Lidia Standish, testifying in connection with a trial for fornication, spoke of herself as "a mother of many children my selfe and have Nursed many." Ms. deposition, in the "Davis Scrapbooks," III, 12, at Pilgrim Hall, Plymouth, Mass.
6. On the question of the relationship between lactation and fertility, see Robert G. Potter et al., "Application of Field Studies to Research on the Physiology of Human Reproduction," in *Journal of Chronic Diseases*, XVIII (1965), 1125–40.
7. There is one alternative explanation for these data which must at least be considered. It is just possible that the settlers maintained a taboo against sexual relations between husband and wife whenever the latter was nursing a child. A custom of this type has been noted among *many* preindustrial peoples in the world today. (For example: the Ojibwa and the Jivaro, among American Indian tribes; the Nuer, the Fang, and the Yoruba, all

We can try to pull together these various bits of evidence bearing on infancy as customarily experienced in the Old Colony. And in doing so, we are left with the impression—no stronger word could be justified—that for his first year or so a baby had a relatively comfortable and tranquil time. The ebb and flow of domestic life must have been constantly around him: large families in small houses created an inevitable sense of intimacy. Often he must have been set close to the fireside for warmth. His clothing was light and not especially restrictive, yet the covers laid over him heightened his sense of protection. And most important, he had regular access to his mother's breast [8]—with all that this implies in the way of emotional reassurance, quite apart from the matter of sound physical nourishment. Illness was, of course, a real danger; the death rate for infants under one year seems to have been substantially higher than for any later age. But this fact may well have encouraged an attitude of particular concern and tenderness towards infants.

All such statements are highly conjectural, and so too is any impression we may try to form of the subsequent phases of a child's life. Still, with this strong word of warning, it seems worth proceeding somewhat further. Let us return once again to the writings of John Robinson, for a most arresting pronouncement on the requirements of the child by way of discipline: "And surely there is in all children . . . a stubborness, and stoutness of

---

of Africa; the Trobriands and Samoans, in Oceania.) Specific documentation can be obtained by consulting the appropriate category (#853) in the Human Relations Area File. There is no evidence for such a practice in any European culture of the seventeenth century; but this is not the kind of thing that would likely show up either in written comment from the period, or in secondary works by modern historians.

8. Admittedly, to put it this way skirts one very important question: what *sort* of feeding schedule the infant experiences. It makes considerable difference, of course, both for his immediate comfort and for his later development whether (1) he can obtain the breast simply by crying out for it, or (2) his mother adheres to a firm timetable of feedings at fixed intervals, regardless of his own demands. But there is simply no way of ascertaining what was the usual practice in Plymouth Colony.

mind arising from natural pride, which must, in the first place, be broken and beaten down; that so the foundation of their education being laid in humility and tractableness, other virtues may, in their time, be built thereon... For the beating, and keeping down of this stubborness parents must provide carefully... that the children's wills and wilfulness be restrained and repressed, and that, in time; lest sooner than they imagine, the tender sprigs grow to that stiffness, that they will rather break than bow. Children should not know, if it could be kept from them, that they have a will in their own, but in their parents' keeping; neither should these words be heard from them, save by way of consent, 'I will' or 'I will not'." [9]

Translated into the language of modern psychology this statement amounts to a blanket indictment of the child's strivings toward self-assertion, and particularly of any impulses of direct aggression. The terms "break" and "beat down" ("destroy" is also used further on) seem to admit of no qualification. Robinson urged, moreover, that this sort of discipline be started very early. It had to be accorded "the first place" in a whole sequence of socialization, because until the child's inherent "stubborness" was thoroughly restrained training in the more positive virtues would not really take hold.

Precisely what age Robinson had in mind here is not clear; but we may suspect that it was somewhere between one and two years. This, at any rate, is the period when *every* child develops the ability to assert his own will far more directly and effectively than was possible earlier. His perceptions of himself as apart from other people grow progressively sharper; his world is for the first time explicitly organized in terms of "I" and "you," "mine" and "yours." He makes rapid progress with muscular control and coordination, and thus gains new power to express all his impulses. Even today, with our much more permissive style of child rear-

9. *The Works of John Robinson*, ed. Robert Ashton (Boston, 1851), I, 246–47.

ing, the second year is a time for establishing limits, and often for the direct clash of wills between parent and child.[10] In all likelihood these first raw strivings of the infant self seemed to sincere Puritans a clear manifestation of original sin—the "fruit of natural corruption and root of actual rebellion against God and man," as Robinson himself put it. Such being the case, the only appropriate response from parents was a repressive one.

And there was more still. The second year of life was for many children bounded at either end by experiences of profound loss. Somewhere near its beginning, we have surmised, the child was likely to be weaned; and near its end the arrival of a new baby might be expected. All this would serve to heighten the crisis imposed by the crushing of the child's assertive and aggressive drives.

The pattern is striking in itself; but it gains added significance when set alongside an important theme in the *adult* life of the colonists—namely the whole atmosphere of contention, of chronic and sometimes bitter enmity, to which we have already alluded.[11] This point merits the strongest possible emphasis, because it serves to call in question some extremely venerable and widespread notions about Puritanism. It has long been assumed that the people of this time and culture were peculiarly concerned—were effectively "neurotic," if you will—about all aspects of sex. But there is now a growing body of evidence to the contrary (some of which will be examined shortly); and it might even be argued that the

10. These few sentences represent the briefest summary of a huge psychological literature. For a useful introduction to this literature, see Paul H. Mussen, John J. Conger, and Jerome Kagan, *Child Development and Personality* (New York, 2nd ed., 1963), ch. 7. The same overall viewpoint is apparent in a number of popular books as well—most notably, perhaps, in Dr. Benjamin Spock's famous *Baby and Child Care* (New York, 1945). And finally I would like to acknowledge a special debt in this connection to Alison Demos, age twenty-one months, for a vivid *personal* demonstration of "autonomy" and related themes. Any parent of a child about this age will know what I mean.

11. See above, p. 49.

Puritans took sex more nearly in their stride than most later generations of Americans.[12] Perhaps, though, there was a *different* bugbear in their lives—and psyches—namely, a tight cluster of anxieties about aggression. To read the records of Plymouth, and also those of the other New England settlements, is to sense a very special sort of preoccupation with any overt acts of this character. Here, it seems, was the one area of emotional and interpersonal life about which the Puritans were most concerned, confused, conflicted.

John Robinson's thoughts are pertinent once again, right at this point. His *Works* contain a number of short essays dealing successively with each of the most basic human instincts and emotions; and the one entitled "Of Anger" stands out in a very special way. Robinson could find nothing at all to say in favor of anger—no circumstance which could ever truly justify its expression, no perspective from which its appearance was less than totally repellent. The imagery which he summoned to describe it is intensely vivid. Anger, he wrote, "God so brands, as he scarce doth any created affection"; for it "hath always evil in it." The "wrathful man" is like a "hideous monster," with "his eyes burning, his lips fumbling, his face pale, his teeth gnashing, his mouth foaming, and other parts of his body trembling, and shaking." [13]

But anger, of course, is not easily avoided: efforts to suppress it can succeed only partially and at a very considerable cost. This leads us back to the opening stages in the life of a Puritan child. If his experience was, first, a year or so of general indulgence, and then a radical turn towards severe discipline—if, in particular, his earliest efforts at self-assertion were met with a crushing counterforce—it should not be surprising to find that aggression was a theme of special potency in the culture at large. Patterns of this

12. The only useful study of this matter is Edmund Morgan, "The Puritans and Sex," *New England Quarterly*, XV (1942), 591–607.
13. *The Works of John Robinson*, I, 226.

kind are usually mediated, to a great extent, by fundamental practices and commitments in the area of child-rearing.[14] The latter create what psychologists call a "fixation." Some essential part of the child's personality becomes charged with strong feelings of guilt, anxiety, fear—and fascination. And later experiences cannot completely erase these trends.

The developmental theory of Erik Erikson, more directly applied, helps to fill out this picture: it suggests quite powerfully certain additional lines of connection between infant experience and Puritan character structure. The time between one and two years forms the second stage in Erikson's larger developmental sequence, and he joins its characteristic behaviors under the general theme of "autonomy." "This stage," he writes, "becomes decisive for the ratio between love and hate, for that between freedom of self-expression and its suppression." Further: while the goal of this stage is autonomy, its negative side—its specific vulnerability—is the possibility of lasting "shame and doubt." It is absolutely vital that the child receive support in "his wish to 'stand on his own feet' lest he be overcome by that sense of having exposed himself prematurely and foolishly which we call shame, or that secondary mistrust, that 'double-take,' which we call doubt." If a child does not get this type of support—if, indeed, his efforts to assert himself are firmly "beaten down"—then a considerable preoccupation with shame can be expected in later life as well. At just this point the evidence on the Puritans makes a striking fit; for considerations of shame (and of "face-saving"—its other side) loom very large in a number of areas of their culture. Such considerations are manifest, for example, throughout the legion of Court cases that had to do with personal disputes and rivalries. Many of these cases involved suits for slander or defamation—

14. There is an enormous literature in anthropology, tending to bear out this point of view. And among anthropologists it is particularly associated with the work of the so-called "culture and personality" school. See, for example, Abram Kardiner, *The Psychological Frontiers of Society* (New York, 1945).

where the issue of public exposure, the risk of shame, was absolutely central. Moreover, when a conviction was obtained, the defendant was normally required to withdraw his slanderous statements, and to apologize for them, *in public*. Note, too, that a common punishment, for many different types of offense, was a sentence to "sit in the stocks." Presumably the bite here was the threat of general ridicule.

A second point, more briefly: Erikson contends that each of man's early stages can be fundamentally related to a particular institutional principle. And for the stage we are now discussing he cites "the principle of *law and order*, which in daily life as well as in the high courts of law apportions to each his privileges and his limitations, his obligations and his rights." Surely few people have shown as much concern for "law and order" as the Puritans.[15]

Once established in the manner outlined above, the same style of parental discipline was probably maintained with little significant change for quite a number of years. The average child made his adjustments to it and became fully absorbed into the larger pattern of domestic life. With several older siblings on hand (or younger ones to come) he attracted no special attention. What concessions may have been made to his youth, what his playthings were, and what his games—if any—there is no way of knowing. All such details are hidden from us. As noted previously, however, the fact that children were dressed like adults does seem to imply a whole attitude of mind. The young boy appeared as a miniature of his father, and the young girl as a miniature of her mother. There was no idea that each generation required separate

15. The material contained in these two paragraphs is drawn particularly from Erik Erikson, *Identity and the Life Cycle* (New York, 1959), 65–74. Re "shame" in Puritan child-rearing, note the following attributed to John Ward in Cotton Mather, *Magnalia Christi Americana* (Hartford, 1853), I, 522: "Of young persons he would himself give this advice: 'Whatever you do, be sure to maintain shame in them; for if that be once gone, there is no hope that they'll ever come to good.'" I am indebted to Nancy Falik for bringing this passage to my attention.

spheres of work or recreation.[16] Children learned the behavior appropriate to their sex and station by sharing in the activities of their parents. Habits of worship provide a further case in point: the whole family went to the same Church service, and the young no less than the old were expected to digest the learned words that flowed from the pulpit.

Yet this picture needs one significant amendment: it probably did *not* apply to the very earliest period of childhood. There is, for example, some evidence of a distinctive type of dress for children of less than six or seven years old.[17] Until this age boys and girls seem to have been clothed alike, in a kind of long robe which opened down the front. This garment, while generally similar to the customary dress of grown women, was set off by one curious feature: a pair of ribbons hanging from the back of the shoulders. The switch from this to the "adult" style of dress was quite a symbolic step, and must have been perceived as such by the children themselves.

One other kind of material bearing on the same aspect of development comes from the contracts of apprenticeship (or just plain "service"). Many of these applied to very young children—young, that is, by the standards which we might think appropriate. Six to eight seems to have been the most common age for such arrangements in Plymouth Colony. Here, then, we find a kind of convergence of the evidence, alerting us to the likelihood that the culture attached a very special importance to this particular time of life. Further "proof" is lacking,[18] but perhaps it was now that children began to assume the role of little adults. After all, if ap-

16. A word of caution must be entered here. It is quite possible that certain tasks around the house or farm were normally left to children—that, in short, there was some notion of "children's work." No concrete evidence survives; but if this was the case, it would indicate at least a limited recognition of difference between the child and the adult. Still, the basic lines of contrast relative to the pattern prevalent in our own period remain firm.
17. Earle, *Child Life in Colonial Days*, 41, 44. And, for an extended discussion of the same practice in Europe at this time, see Philippe Aries, *Centuries of Childhood*, trans. Robert Baldick (New York, 1962), ch. 3.
18. Perhaps, though, there is a relevant datum in the Court's handling of bastardy cases. The usual practice was to oblige the father of an illegitimate

prentices and servants were considered able to begin to work effectively at the age of six or seven, it seems reasonable to think that the same judgment might apply to children who remained at home.

In psychological terms there is nothing surprising about any of this. Indeed the culture was reacting in an intuitive way to inherent developmental changes that are widely recognized by behavioral scientists of our own time. A substantial body of recent research on "cognitive development" treats the period from six to eight years as a vital crux. The child leaves behind the disordered and "magical" impressions that characterize his earliest years and becomes for the first time capable of "logical thinking." He begins, for example, to understand cause and effect, and other such abstract relationships.[19] Emotionally, too, there are changes of great magnitude. According to psychoanalytic theory this is the period when the child effects a massive repression of his oedipal wishes for the parent of the opposite sex. He does so, in part, by identifying with the parent of the *same* sex—by trying, in short, to imitate various aspects of adult behavior and style.[20] More gen-

child to pay a certain sum each week for maintenance, over a period of six or seven years. What would happen *after* this time is never indicated, but possibly it was felt that the child would then be able to earn his own keep, either in helping his mother and her family or in being "put out" to some foster family. See, for example, the case of Rebecca Littlefield vs. Israel Woodcock, *Plymouth Colony Records*, V, 161; and that of Elizabeth Woodward vs. Robert Stedson, *ibid.*, V, 181. Edmund Morgan, in *The Puritan Family* (New York, 1966), 66, calls attention to a statement by John Cotton that is also interesting in this connection. Cotton believed that it was perfectly normal for very young children to "spend much time in pastime and play, for their bodyes are too weak to labour, and their mind to study are too shallow . . . even the first seven years are spent in pastime, and God looks not much at it."

19. This is a central theme in many studies of cognitive psychology; but it is associated, above all, with the work of Jean Piaget. See, for example, Barbel Inhelder and Jean Piaget, *The Growth of Logical Thinking from Childhood to Adolescence*, trans. Anne Parsons and Stanley Milgram (New York, 1958).

20. Of course, the Oedipus complex has an absolutely central place in the whole psychoanalytic scheme, and the writings which deal with it are legion. But for a good short summary, see Otto Fenichel, *The Psychoanalytic Theory of Neurosis* (New York, 1945), chs. V, VI.

erally, he wishes to "learn to accomplish things which one would never have thought of by oneself, things which owe their attractiveness to the very fact that they are *not* the product of play and fantasy but the product of reality, practicality, and logic; things which thus provide a token sense of participation in the real world of adults." [21]

Virtually all cultures accord some special recognition to this stage of development. In complex (and literate) societies like our own it is the usual time for beginning school. Among "primitive" peoples the child starts now to master "the basic skills of technology"; he learns "to handle the utensils, the tools, and the weapons used by the big people: he enters the technology of his tribe very gradually but also very directly." [22] Naturally, this too is an important kind of "instruction," which capitalizes on the child's new mental and emotional capacities

In this respect Plymouth probably was closest to the model of the primitive cultures. The training that began at the age of six or seven was, it seems, chiefly of a "technological" kind. The boy starting to work with his father at planting or fencemending, and the girl helping her mother with cooking or spinning or candlemaking, were both learning to master "the utensils, the tools, and the weapons used by the big people." But this society was at least partially literate, and it is possible that some training of a more academic sort was also begun about now. Perhaps there was a new intensity in the religious tutelage or "catechizing" provided for children; and perhaps they began to learn the "three R's." Unfortunately, however, such questions can be raised only in a speculative way since the historical record becomes at this point quite mute.[23]

But what of education in a more formal sense? Were there no

---

21. Erikson, *Identity and the Life Cycle*, 84.
22. *Ibid.*, 83.
23. Or at least there is no evidence for Plymouth. The case seems otherwise for Massachusetts Bay. Morgan's *Puritan Family*, 96 ff., quotes some interesting statements by various Massachusetts clergymen on the subject of the religious instruction of the child. The statements imply a rather

bona fide schools for the children of Plymouth? A brief answer to this question would have to be negative, at least if one thinks in overall terms for the whole of the Old Colony period. For the first forty odd years of settlement there is only indirect evidence of the intent to found schools,[24] and no evidence at all of schools in actual operation. Later on, admittedly, the picture did start to change. In December of 1670, for example, John Morton appeared before the Plymouth town meeting and "proffered to teach the children and youth of the towne to Reade and write and Cast accounts on Reasonable considerations." [25] The following year he renewed his proposal and the townsmen responded with a plan to raise money "for and toward the Maintenance of the free Scoole now begun and erected." [26] Meanwhile the General Court was taking similar steps on a Colony-wide basis. A fishing excise was to be allocated to any towns that could show a school actually underway.[27] In 1673 this money was awarded to Plymouth. In 1681 it went partly to Rehoboth and partly to "Mr Ichabod Wiswalls schoole at Duxburrow." In 1683 it was distributed among five different towns: Barnstable, Duxbury, Taunton, Rehoboth, and Bristol.[28]

Thus the trend in these later years was generally in the direction of increased facilities for formal schooling. Yet not until long afterward—well into the eighteenth century—would it produce a really firm and widespread system. The town of Plymouth itself

---

limited and fragmentary approach to the youngest children, followed later on by a switch to a more intense and systematic program. They do not indicate the precise age at which this switch was appropriate, but one is tempted to make a guess of six or seven. And what was true of the one Puritan colony was likely also to be true of its Puritan neighbor, Plymouth.
24. The Marshfield Town Records show that at a meeting in 1645 there was discussion of a proposal to raise money "for one to teach school." Ms. collections, Clerk's Office, Marshfield, Mass. See also John A. Goodwin, *The Pilgrim Republic* (Boston, 1888), 494–95. Goodwin cites some early indications of an intent to found schools which I have not been able to trace.
25. *Records of the Town of Plymouth* (Plymouth, 1889), I, 115.
26. *Ibid.*, 124.
27. *Plymouth Colony Records*, V, 107–8.
28. *Ibid.*, 108; VI, 81; VI, 102–3.

can be cited to illustrate the point. Its achievement in starting a school during the 1670s was apparently not sustained, for two decades later its citizens repeatedly went on record with directives that the selectmen "should Indeavor to get A scoolmaster to teach Children to Reade and write." [29] Education under these conditions was definitely a sometime thing.

The whole subject of education in the American colonies was somewhat misconceived until a fascinating essay by Bernard Bailyn (published in 1960) supplied a new and much more meaningful focus.[30] Bailyn was the first to point out that formal schools constituted only a small part of the total educational process, at least with the first generations of settlers. Indeed they formed a kind of appendage to other, far more important and more comprehensive agencies: the church, the community at large, and above all the family itself. This situation was to change radically before the end of the colonial period, owing to the corrosive effects of the New World environment on Old World habits and institutions. By the time of the Revolution the web of connections between family, church, and community was irrevocably broken, and schools were increasingly called upon to fill a part of the resultant social void.

But only the first part of Bailyn's story seems relevant to Plymouth Colony. To be sure, there were certain glimmerings of the cultural disruption to which he ascribes such importance; and near the end of the Colony's lifetime the process of institutionalizing education, the proliferation of schools, was clearly under way. But for most children of this period and place the major kinds of learning occurred at home. Here, in the context of the total household environment, values, manners, literacy, vocation were all transmitted from one generation to the next. The process was none the less real for being only partly conscious.

29. *Records of the Town of Plymouth*, I, 224, 245.
30. Bernard Bailyn, *Education in the Forming of American Society* (Chapel Hill, N.C., 1960).

CHAPTER TEN

COMING OF AGE

ᔐᔒ

It is striking that the seventeenth century (indeed all centuries before our own) had no real word for the period of life between
puberty and full manhood. The term "adolescence" is little
more than seventy-five years old, at least in the sense of having a
wide currency.[1] Earlier the word "youth" might be used for
many purposes, but its boundaries in time and its inner meaning
were seemingly quite vague. These semantic details point to a
very substantial area of contrast in the developmental process as
experienced then and now. Our own view of adolescence as a
time of "storm and stress," of deep inner conflict, of uncertainty

1. Very little research on the history of adolescence has been published as
yet. But there is not much doubt that the word—and the fact—are far more
important to the twentieth than to any previous century. The first great
student of adolescence was the psychologist G. Stanley Hall; and it was he
who gave the topic a wide public currency as well, with his encyclopedic
work, *Adolescence: Its Psychology, and Its Relations to Physiology, Anthropology, Sociology, Sex, Crime, Religion and Education* (New York,
1904). For a general discussion of Hall's work, and the "discovery" of adolescence, see John Demos and Virginia Demos, "Adolescence in Historical
Perspective," *Journal of Marriage and the Family*, XXXI (1969), No. 4.

and rebelliousness, needs no discussion here. But it does provide a convenient starting point from which to reconstruct the rather different set of assumptions that must have obtained among the people of the Old Colony.

The evidence on this matter is in a sense largely negative: one looks for signs of a difficult adolescence in the sources from the period, and looks in vain. For instance, nothing in the Court records suggests any particular problems of law enforcement connected with this stage of life. There was certainly no institution comparable to our own juvenile courts—and apparently no "juvenile delinquency." Moreover, the Church Records are equally uninformative. It is well known that during the nineteenth century religious "conversions" occurred most typically among young people in their teens; [2] but no similar pattern can be uncovered for the Old Colony. (Many Puritan conversions seem to have occurred well before puberty.[3] Perhaps, indeed, a religious "crisis" can more reasonably be connected with the whole matrix of changes customary for children at the age of about six to eight.)

We might examine, also, another matter of some interest to recent scholars of Puritanism: [4] the process whereby young people found a "calling" to a specific occupation. Perhaps *here* one can establish a firm link with adolescence? But several considerations stand in the way of this hypothesis. First, it is quite unclear what part of the total population was ever seriously preoccupied with the selection of a suitable calling. There are, for Massachusetts, literary materials (sermons, essays, and so forth) which bear directly on this subject, and which do argue a kind of intellectual concern among men of high social and economic status. But no similar evidence exists that would take in average people as well.

2. See, for example, E. D. Starbuck, *The Psychology of Religion* (New York, 1899).
3. For some rather fragmentary evidence on this point, see Fleming, *Children and Puritanism*, 127–45; and Earle, *Child Life in Colonial Days*, 250–51. The issue is, however, hardly settled one way or the other, and I offer the above simply as a suggestion.
4. For example, Morgan, *The Puritan Family*, 67–75.

We noted earlier that most contracts of apprenticeship and servitude were quite vague about the actual work to be performed or learned. Recall, for instance, the two agreements for "putting out" young Benjamin Savory—the first directing that he learn "whatsoever trad his master . . . can Doe," the second that he be taught "in learning that is to say to read and write and . . . in husbandry."[5] After all, the range of occupational possibilities confronting a young man in this period was quite limited—in dramatic contrast to the situation prevailing today. The professional and "artisan" classes were relatively small, and the vast majority of the populace was engaged simply in farming. In the typical case, therefore, the choice of a calling was scarcely a choice at all; instead it was something assumed, something everywhere implicit in the child's surroundings and in the whole process of growth. Finally, there is the matter of the age at which service or apprenticeship might begin. Even in those instances where the learning of a particular trade *was* specified, the child involved was often as young as six or seven.

In some cultures a crisis at adolescence is mediated by vivid symbolic observances. "Initiation rites," or other ceremonies of a less formal type, mark a certain point in time as the boundary between childhood and maturity, and help to smooth the transition. (In our own society graduation exercises might be regarded as a weak sort of functional equivalent.) But nothing of this kind can be traced for Plymouth. In fact, the extant materials imply a nearly opposite case—an understanding of growth which explicitly recognized a series of partial steps and changes. The pattern appears most clearly in the arrangement of legal privileges and responsibilities. Thus an orphaned child was allowed to make his own choice of "guardians" when he reached the age of fourteen.[6] The laws against lying and slander were written so as

5. See above, p. 72.
6. See William Brigham, *The Compact with the Charter and Laws of the Colony of New Plymouth* (Boston, 1836), 255.

to apply to all persons "of the age of discretion which is ac-
counted sixteene yeares." [7] Sixteen was also the age at which
boys became liable for military duty.[8]

Two other matters of importance here—political participation
and inheritance customs—cannot be described with quite the same
degree of precision. The status of "freeman" conferred the right
to take part in the government of the Colony as a whole; and
scholars have generally associated it with the attainment of a majority in our own sense, that is, with the age of twenty-one years.
But the point was never established officially until the broad revi-
sion of the Colony laws in 1671,[9] and twenty-one would in any
case represent only a minimum. What, then, of actual *practice* in
this regard? An examination of some sixty persons for whom
there is sufficient data shows clearly that no set age brought
admission to freemanship. The sample spreads out across a broad
range from twenty-five to forty, with some tendency to cluster
in the early thirties. This privilege and responsbility (for it
was both) was perhaps the last in the series of steps leading to full
adult citizenship in the community.

But freemanship and the right to participate in *local* government (each individual town) seem not to have coincided; and it is
quite possible that the latter would come much earlier in a man's
life, perhaps even before the age of twenty-one. There is, at any
rate, one puzzling little notation in the Colony Records—a decree
issued by the General Court during the year 1667 which reads as
follows: "In reference to milletary concernments It is enacted by
the Court that noe single psons under twenty yeares of age either
children or servants shall voate as to that accompt." [10] Just what
did this mean? Since there were no freemen as young as twenty, it
cannot have referred to the Court's own deliberations. Perhaps,
then, it applied to actions which the towns might take individu-

7. *Ibid.*, 98.
8. *Ibid.*, 285–86.
9. *Ibid.*, 258.
10. *Plymouth Colony Records*, XI, 219.

ally for their defense. Or perhaps it applied to elective procedures within the military units themselves. In either case it suggests still another demarcation point within the larger course of development.

The age of inheritance for children whose father had died while they were still relatively young was usually stipulated by will. A clause in the will of John Huckens of Barnstable was quite typical: his five children would receive their portions "as they or any of them shall attaine the age of twenty one yeers Respectively or the Day of Marriage which shall first happen." [11] Twenty-one was the age most often specified, but a father was free to do as he pleased in any particular instance. Nearly all of the alternatives that can actually be documented fall on the *younger* side of twenty-one. The will of Alexander Winchester, written in 1647, supplies a kind of minimum case: he left half of his property to his widow, and the other half to be divided among the children "equaly to each of them when they shall come to the age of fiveteene yeares." [12] Samuel Fuller transferred to his overseers the power to decide on the actual timing of his bequests: "I would have [my children] enjoy that smale porcon the Lord shall give them when my Overseers thinke them to be of fit discretion & not at any set time or appointmt of yeares." [13]

All of this is meant to suggest the fluidity, the range of gradations that the culture presented to children on their way to becoming adults. It may now be useful to introduce certain more theoretical considerations as a way of drawing the discussion together in one broad interpretive framework. Adolescence has, in every life, a real and important biological foundation: sexual maturation is only the most dramatic of a whole set of profound internal changes. But the matter of context—what a given society *does* with and about these changes—is highly variable. What ap-

11. *Mayflower Descendant*, XXIV, 180.
12. *Mayflower Descendant*, IX, 30.
13. *Mayflower Descendant*, I, 27.

pears as a crisis in one setting may wear a much more placid aspect in another. In cultures where a prolonged period of adolescent crisis *is*, more or less, a normal part of development two kinds of social factors seem broadly responsible: (1) There are major "discontinuities" between the generations; the common experiences of children and adults are radically different from one another. (2) The culture itself is enormously varied and complex. Thus the young person approaching adulthood confronts a bewildering array of alternatives as to career, values, life style, and so forth. In this overall context adolescence brings a deeply rooted cluster of fears and resentments, and a host of ominous questions: "Can I effectively bridge the gap?" "Will I be able to make the right basic choices?" "Or, for that matter, do I *want* to?" [14]

In Plymouth, by contrast, and indeed in all communities of the seventeenth century, the environmental setting was much simpler—and the process of growth inherently less difficult. Once the child had begun to assume an adult role and style, around the age of six or seven, the way ahead was fairly straightforward. Development toward full maturity could be accomplished in a gradual, piecemeal, and largely automatic fashion. There were few substantial choices to be made; the boy's own father, or the girl's own mother, provided relatively clear models for the formation of a meaningful "identity." Here was no "awkward age"—but rather the steady lengthening of a young person's shadow, and the whole instinctive process through which one generation yielded imperceptibly to its successor.

Most of the wills from the Old Colony, including some of those already examined here, specified as the time for inheritance a par-

14. This paragraph represents the briefest sort of summary of a vast body of recent writing on adolescence. See, for example, Kenneth Keniston, "Social Change and Youth in America," *Daedalus* (Winter, 1962), 145–71; Erik H. Erikson, "Youth: Fidelity and Diversity," *Daedalus* (Winter, 1962), 5–27; and Ruth Benedict, "Continuities and Discontinuities in Cultural Conditioning," *Psychiatry*, I, 161–67.

ticular age *or* the beginning of marriage. They suggest, therefore, that marriage could provide a means of short-circuiting some of the later steps on the road to adulthood. But how often did it actually work out this way?

The average age at marriage in this period was, in fact, much higher than has usually been imagined. For men the figure ranged gradually downward from about twenty-seven years at the time of settlement to a little under twenty-five by the end of the Old Colony period. For women the average was just over twenty at the start, and rose during the same span to around twenty-two.[15] These changes over time, and in particular the opposite trends of the sexes, reflected an important shift in the Colony's overall sex ratio. Men greatly outnumbered women among the first waves of settlers, but as the years passed this imbalance corrected itself. Thus for men it became progressively easier to find a spouse, and for women progressively more difficult. But the important point is this: the average age at marriage was for the most part higher than the accepted age of inheritance (twenty-one or less). The only contrary case was that of women who lived during the early part of our period, and even there it was a narrow thing. With the men the situation was quite clear-cut throughout: in virtually every case inheritance preceded marriage, and usually by several years.

Yet so far we have been considering only one kind of evidence, formal bequests legally specified by will; and this means that our conclusions can apply only to people who were orphaned as children. What can be said of the many others, surely a much larger group, who reached maturity with parents, or at least fathers, very much alive? This is an extremely troublesome question; indeed no final or definitive answer can be given. But nothing is more essential to a real understanding of the inner workings of seventeenth-century families, and the subject deserves, at the very least, some fairly extended discussion.

15. See Appendix, Table IV.

Let us try to construct a picture of the whole process of making a marriage, starting as far back as the evidence will allow. What basic steps and procedures were involved? And what did it all mean, how was it experienced, from the standpoint of the individuals directly concerned and of the community at large?

The initial phases of courtship must, unfortunately, be passed over with barely a word said, for they are nearly invisible from this distance in time. Probably they lacked much formal ceremony (no dating, dances, and so forth). Probably they showed close connections to other aspects of everyday life, to common patterns of work and leisure. Probably too they developed under the watchful eye of parents and siblings, or indeed of a whole neighborhood. (Sustained privacy is hard to imagine, in *any* part of the Old Colony setting.) But all this is very much in the realm of speculation.

It is worth noting, however, that some Plymouth courtships fell considerably short of "Puritanical" standards—and here the Court Records do supply certain pieces of concrete evidence. There was, throughout the century, a steady succession of trials and convictions for sexual offenses involving single persons. "Fornication," in particular, was a familiar problem. There is no way to measure its incidence in quantitative terms, but it happened, and happened with some regularity. The punishment for fornication was pretty standard—a fine of ten pounds, or a public whipping —and applied equally to both parties.[16] When such acts became known and liable to prosecution, it was usually because a pregnancy had resulted. Occasionally the girl involved would refuse to reveal her lover's identity, but this decision laid her open to a particularly trying little ordeal. For when delivery was actually in progress and the girl's powers of resistance were presumed to be at their lowest ebb, the midwives were likely to "charge it upon her . . . to tell whose the child was." [17] The au-

16. *Plymouth Colony Records,* XI, 46.
17. As reported in the case of Martha Hewitt, *Plymouth Colony Records,* V, 14.

thorities wished to discover the father in these cases, in order to punish him and to make him financially responsible for his child's maintenance. (Otherwise the community as a whole might be obliged to assume this expense, especially if the mother had few resources of her own.) Often, though, a woman who became pregnant out of wedlock was more than ready to name her partner: feelings of jealousy, or resentment at being abandoned, found an easy outlet in open testimony before the Court.[18] But the man himself might contest such allegations, and the Court might eventually decide to let him off.[19] There are numerous paternity cases in the Records, and some of them seem very complicated indeed.

When all of these materials are brought together it becomes difficult to sustain the traditional picture of seventeenth-century New England as being extremely strait-laced and repressive in anything pertaining to sex. And there is additional, confirming evidence. Consider, for example, certain trial records in cases of defamation and slander—records which suggest that sexual gossip, while surely not condoned, was an unavoidable part of the larger social atmosphere. The following official statement of apology, ordered by the Court (and entered in its records) was not in any sense unusual: "Whereas I, Abraham Peirce, Junir, haue follishly and unadvisedly reported to Ruth Sprague and Bethyah Tubbs, at the house of Francies Sprague, that Rebeckah Alden and Hester Delanoy were withchild, and thereupon wee should have young troopers within three quarters of a yeare, I doe freely and from my hart owne my fault heerin, and am hartily sorry that I have so spooken, to theire great reproch and wronge and the defamation of their relations." [20] Consider, too, a deposition by one "Jarvis" in a paternity case of 1686. Entitled "Evidences about Joseoph Boelk and Mary Sutton", it states "that I have many times seene owen Rilly and marry sutton very fammilier together & I further

18. See, for example, the cases involving Mary Churchill (*Plymouth Colony Records*, V, 83) and Elizabeth Loe (*ibid.*, 160).
19. *Plymouth Colony Records*, IV, 7.
20. *Ibid.*, 7.

testifie that I asked George Hollyster why hee got mary sutton with child & hee said it is mine." [21] What shall we make of this? Was Mary Sutton so promiscuous that four different men(Boelk, Rilly, Hollyster, and Jarvis himself) could be suspected of having fathered her child?

Regardless how common or uncommon such episodes may have been, they clearly belonged to a category of behavior which the community opposed. But let us return now to the standard, *approved* procedures leading up to marriage. First of all, and most important: when a courtship had developed to a certain point of intensity, the parents became directly involved. An early order of the General Court directed that "none be allowed to marry that are under the covert of parents but by their consent and approbacon." [22] Later on, the Court came to feel that a stronger statement was necessary and amended the law to read as follows: "If any shall make any motion of marriage to any mans daughter or mayde servant not haveing first obtayned leave and consent of the parents or master so to doe [he] shalbe punished either by fine or corporall punishment or both." [23]

We cannot discover in any detail how parents and masters would evaluate a particular "motion of marriage," but some of the Court's own assumptions were explicitly stated. In a kind of preamble to the above legislation it deplored the actions of "divers persons unfitt for marriage both in regard of their yeong yeares as also in regard of theire weake estate" in "practising the enveagleing" of various "daughters &...mayde servants" in the Colony.[24] Marriage by the very young or the very poor seemed a dubious proposition to men in authority. Occasionally a personal document indicates something of the same type of concern. When Nathaniel Warren wrote his will in 1667, he included a

21. Ms. deposition in the "Davis Scrapbooks," III, 7, at Pilgrim Hall, Plymouth, Mass.
22. Brigham, *The Compact with the Charter and Laws of the Colony of New Plymouth*, 44.
23. *Ibid.*, 61.
24. *Ibid.*

formal request to his overseers "to advise about and take Care of my Children in reference to theire marriage; That they bee matched with such as may be fitt for them both in reference to theire spirituall and outward estate." [25] An appearance of "fitness," in this broad double sense, must have been a fundamental criterion for the great majority of parents.

In theory at least, there were some limits on the power of parents and masters to decide such questions. The law recognized that certain men might refuse their consent to "a meet Marriage . . . orderly proposed," out of some "sinister end, or covetous desire"; and it authorized an appeal in such cases to the local magistrates "to determine . . . as they judge equal between both parties." [26] But in actual fact, actions of this type were rarely, if ever, initiated. Indeed the reverse situation is what shows up in the Colony records—the situation in which a father sought to forestall an attempt to woo his daughter contrary to his own wishes. The most famous case grew out of a romance between Elizabeth Prence, daughter of the Governor, and Arthur Howland, Jr. The Court heard several complaints about the matter and decided, in 1667, to fine Howland £5 "for inveigling of Mistris Elizabeth Prence and makeing motion of marriage to her, and procecuting the same contrary to her parents likeing, and without theire consent, and directly contrary to theire mind and will." [27] Howland had earlier converted to Quakerism—a faith which many in the Old Colony regarded as dangerously heretical—and probably this was the objection to his suit of Mistress Prence. But Howland would not give up, and in 1668 the Governor apparently decided to relent. That spring, at last, the couple was married—ending three long years of disappointment and frustration.[28]

25. *Mayflower Descendant*, II, 38.
26. Brigham, *The Compact with the Charter and Laws of the Colony of New Plymouth*, 272.
27. *Plymouth Colony Records*, IV, 140.
28. For a similar case, but involving a master's refusal to consent to "a mocion of marriage" made to his servant girl, see *Plymouth Colony Records*, III, 5 ("presentment" of Jonathan Countrey of Marshfield).

Court cases like this one were relatively infrequent, and it may be that informal sanctions and pressures were more important in the long run. The wills, for example, suggest that a parent's control of property and his power to dictate the terms of an inheritance gave him considerable leverage in these situations. One man left his daughter a handsome gift of household furnishings "att her marriage and if shee please her mother in her match." [29] Another willed the bulk of his property to his four sons, with this proviso: "that att what time all or any of my said sonnes; are or shalbe Disposed to marry; they each one for him selfe, shall advise therin with, and have the Consent of all or the Major prte of the said overseers then surviveing; upon penalty of being by them Disinherited." [30] A bit more of the human detail implicit in these situations can be teased out of a complicated set of testimonies bearing on the settlement of the estate of a certain widow Abigail Young. Two sons, named Robert and Henry, were her most likely heirs; but the claims of the former were challenged almost immediately. A third son (Joseph) reported that "when shee dyed [she said] shee would Leave all ye estate that shee had with Henry, if Robart had that gierl that there was a discourse about: but if he had her not I understood that the estate should be devided betweix them." And a fourth (Nathaniel) confirmed this: "My mother young told me that if Robirt had that gierl which there was a talke about shee would not give him a peny." [31] It seems, then, that the desire of a young person to make his own choice of courtship partners *could* generate considerable conflict with his parents.

But these were more or less aberrant cases, and it is necessary once again to pull the discussion back to the area of conduct regarded at the time as normal and desirable. Assume that a particular couple had recognized a mutual attraction, had courted for a

29. *Mayflower Descendant*, XV, 235.
30. *Mayflower Descendant*, XI, 82.
31. *Ibid.*, 79–80.

reasonable interval, had shown at least outward conformance to the moral code of the community (no embarrassing pregnancy), had secured the approval of both sets of parents and reached a firm decision to marry. What next? In fact, a series of steps remained to be taken, some more and some less formal, but all of them absolutely necessary. There was, for example, the "betrothal" or "contract"—a simple ceremony which bears comparison to our own custom of "engagement." Its meaning was stated as follows in the Colony Records: "by a lawfull contract the Court understands the mutuall consent of two parties with the consent of parents or gaurdians if there be any to be had and a solemne promise of marriage in due tyme to eich other before two competent witnesses." [32]

To be contracted in this way was a very serious undertaking; and it placed a person in quite a special position—not yet married, but no longer "single" either. Any failure to fulfill such a contract would create the likelihood of legal action, and a damage suit of very considerable proportions. [33] The laws against adultery were written so as to cover married and "betrothed" people in exactly equal measure. [34] On the other hand, sexual intimacies *between*

32. Brigham, *The Compact with the Charter and Laws of the Colony of New Plymouth*, 79-80.
33. A long and complicated case spanning the period 1661–1663 began with a suit for £200 in damages, by John Sutton against Mary Russell "for engaging herselfe to another by promise of marriage wheras shee had engaged herselfe by promise of marriage unto the said John before." An initial judgment in Sutton's favor carried an award of £15 plus the costs of the suit. But later the case was reviewed and the earlier verdict reversed. The court decided that Mary (now married to John Jacob) had "heard such thinges concerning the said Sutton as might justly discourage her"—things, moreover, which constituted "just ground to retract from any such conditionall promise or engagement, as appeered to have bine made by her." Consequently she, and her new husband, were awarded fifty shillings (to be paid by Sutton) for the trouble caused them in all the proceedings. *Plymouth Colony Records*, VIII, 101, 109. For other cases of a similar nature, see *Plymouth Colony Records*, VII, 101 (Richard Sylvester vs. John Palmer, Jr.) and *Plymouth Colony Records*, V, 116 (Richard Sutton vs. Moses Symonds).
34. Brigham, *The Compact with the Charter and Laws of the Colony of New Plymouth*, 245-46.

the contracted parties fell into a category all their own. They could not be officially condoned, but the usual penalty was relatively light—only a fourth of what obtained for the same offense by those who were unequivocally single.[35] The records are sprinkled through with cases of couples who had apparently "slipped" in this way—by being intimate during the period between the contract and the actual marriage. As with cases of ordinary fornication, the only way such misconduct could come to light was through a pregnancy. A pair of newlyweds who produced a child in substantially less than nine months after marriage were liable to immediate prosecution.[36] Of course, there was always the possibility of a premature birth, and in this connection the opinion of midwives and other women present at the delivery was usually decisive. Did the infant look strange? Did it, in short, have the appearance of being premature? (If so, the parents might be fully

35. The prescribed penalty for sexual intercourse "before or without lawfull contract" was a fine of ten pounds for each party, or a public whipping. For the same offense "after contract and before marriage" it was fifty shillings apiece. *Plymouth Colony Records*, XI, 95. It has been suggested elsewhere that this very different scale of punishment may actually have worked to encourage premarital relations among "betrothed" couples. See George Elliott Howard, *A History of Matrimonial Institutions* (Chicago, 1904), II, 169–200. Howard's discussion of marriage customs in colonial New England is, on the whole, quite accurate and useful.
36. Many Court cases of this type could be cited. Usually they show up in the following, simple kind of notation: "Thomas Cushman, for comitting carnall coppulation with his now wife before marriage but after contract, is centanced by the Court to pay five pounds, according to the Law." *Plymouth Colony Records*, IV, 83. (For similar cases, see *Plymouth Colony Records*, I, 12, 93; VI, 115, 201.) The Church was also likely to take action in cases of fornication. Thus, for example, the records of the congregation at Plymouth show this entry for July 13, 1684: "William Shirtliffe was called forthe before the church in the open Assembly, to answer for his sin in carnall fellowship with her whom afterwards he married, his child being borne 26 weekes after marriage; William shewed little sense of sin, the church voted, & the Elder laid him under Admonition, for his sin, & for the pride and hardnesse of his heart." *Plymouth Church Records*, Publications of the Colonial Society of Massachusetts (Boston, 1920), XXII 256. Curiously enough Shirtliffe was never arraigned in any civil action on this account; and it may be that the court did not apply the fornication laws consistently. For similar proceedings in the Plymouth Church, see *ibid.*, 251, 261, 275.

exonerated.) The following sort of testimony was typical: "Lidiah Standish aged fifty five yeares testifieth and saith I beinge at the house of John merrite after his wife was brought a body [?] of her child and I saw the child and by the behavore of the Child I cannot Judg but that the child was borne be fore the mother of the Child had gone her full time I beinge a mother of many Children my selfe and have Nursed many but I never saw none as that... except it weare such which the mother had not gone there full tim with." [37] The final disposition of this case is not recorded, but it may be that with such an "expert" opinion weighing in their favor the Merritts were able to secure an acquittal. Many others were not so fortunate, and it seems possible too that some of them were innocent. Obstetrical practice now recognizes that a certain portion of infants are bound to be premature—some by as much as two months. But the Court of the Old Colony drew the line more finely—witness the prosecution in 1652 of Nicholas Davis and his wife "for haveing a child five weekes and four daies before the ordinary time of weemen after marriage." [38]

Once a contract had been solemnized in the manner described above, another formal step became necessary: the "publishing" of the banns. "For the prevention of unlawful Marriages"—the law stated—"it is ordered, That no person shall be joyned in Marriage, before the intention of the parties proceeding therein hath been published three times at some publick meeting, in the Towns where the parties or either of them do ordinarily reside, or by setting up in writeing, upon some Post of their Meeting house door in publick view, there to stand as it may be easily read, by the space of fourteen dayes." [39]

Another matter, less official but obviously of the greatest im-

37. Ms. deposition in the "Davis Scrapbooks," III, 12, at Pilgrim Hall, Plymouth, Mass.
38. *Plymouth Colony Records*, III, 6. See also the case of Thomas Launders and wife, *ibid*.
39. Brigham, *The Compact with the Charter and Laws of the Colony of New Plymouth*, 272.

portance, was a set of transactions designed to underwrite the economic welfare of the contracted couple. Marriage was in this culture the usual occasion for the transfer from parent to child of a certain substantial "portion" of property. For many people, this represented most or all of the inheritance they would ever receive. There was no simple formula governing the content of a portion: a variety of special circumstances might prove decisive in any individual case. More often than not, however, a young man would receive the bulk of his portion in the form of land and housing, and a woman would be given a variety of domestic furnishings, cattle, and/or money. Usually these arrangements were very detailed, and it may be useful to present some specific cases by way of illustration. A lengthy deed, recorded in June 1646 and entitled "the condicions of the marriage between Jacob Cooke and Damarise hopkins," listed five major "gifts" from Francis Cooke, the groom's father: first, "one hundred acres of land with meddow . . . 2condly . . . halfe the Land that att any time shall fall to him the said ffrancis by any Devision of the Purchase Land or Due to the first commers . . . 3dly . . . one oxe one cow and one calfe and the next fole that the said ffrancis his mare bringeth . . . 4ly It is promised . . . that att any time that the said Jacob shall see most conducable to his condicon . . . [he may] build an house upon the Land wherof the said ffrancis is now possessed of att Rockynooke . . . 5ly . . . att the Decease of the Longer surviver of the said ffrancis and hester [his wife] that then and att such time the said Jacob or his heires shall have the teame with all the furniture belonging therunto." [40]

No precisely comparable deed exists for the properties contributed on behalf of the bride. But two years earlier her father, Stephen Hopkins, had died, and the bulk of his estate was "Devided equally" by his overseers among the surviving children. [41] The items designated as "Damaris porcon" can be taken to represent

40. *Mayflower Descendant*, II, 27–28.
41. *Mayflower Descendant*, IV, 115.

what she was able to bring to her marriage. They seem, moreover, representative of many bride's portions of this period—and hence of the kind and range of domestic equipment with which an average couple would attempt to set up housekeeping. The list reads as follows:

i	feather bed boulster pillow a stray bed a suite of cloathes another pettycote and a beaver muff	04.10.00
i	silver spoone	00.08.00
ii	checker coverings	00.16.00
i	peere of linnen sheets	00.08.00
i	pillow beere	00.03.00
2	napkins & 2 table cloths	00.02.06
i	chest box and a Case	00.08.00
an	Alkemy spoone	00.00.02
i	great Cittell	01.02.00
5	trenchers 2 pewter platters I quart pot i pynt pott i salt 2 porringers i chamber pott i tin candlestick i earthen judg i linke & i sive	00.12.00
i	stoole	00.05.00
	Due for hemp	00.02.00
	for part of a cloake	00.10.00

The last two entries appear to be sums of money, in lieu of the items themselves. The value of the whole inheritance, computed from the figures in the right-hand column, is a little over nine pounds. This seems less than the sum of the various properties promised by the groom's father, but it would not be wise to draw a general inference here. The details of any marriage settlement corresponded to the particular circumstances of the families involved, and the contributions from each side reflected, above all, the ability to pay. Unfortunately, no document from the Old Colony reveals the process of negotiation that must have preceded such agreements. But the diary of Samuel Sewall of Massachusetts

Bay describes some episodes of very tough bargaining in this connection, and one can at least suspect a similar pattern at Plymouth.[42]

As noted already, fourteen days was the minimum interval allowable between the betrothal ceremony and the wedding itself—between "contract" and "covenant," in the language of the time. But in actual fact most couples waited considerable longer: two or three months seems to have been quite customary.[43] Whether or not some contracts were given up by mutual agreement in the meantime we have no way of knowing, for such things would not turn up in any official records. But tradition has it that this was an occasion for sober reflection, and, if need be, for reconsideration—before the final step was taken.

With respect to the actual wedding ceremony the views of the Puritans, and the Pilgrims among them, were most distinctive. They regarded marriage "as being a civil thing" (the words are Bradford's),[44] as an institution of this world that would find no place or parallel in the next. It was, then, not a sacrament, but rather another type of contract between two individual persons, and centrally bound up with questions of ownership, inheritance, residence, and the like. None of this should be thought to imply that the Puritans took marriage lightly; surely, in some broader sense, they viewed it as having many vital interconnections with a whole Godly pattern of life. But still the ceremony was to them a *civil* ceremony, not a religious rite—and was therefore the responsibility of magistrates, not ministers.

The danger implicit in these beliefs was that some men might

42. Morgan provides a rather full account of Sewall's courtships in his *The Puritan Family*.

43. This, at least, is the impression one gains from reading the vital records of the various Old Colony towns. The section of these volumes dealing with "Marriages" contains in many instances a date for the announcement of a couple's "intention" to marry and another date for the actual wedding ceremony. The interval between the two usually works out to two or three months, and occasionally much longer.

44. William Bradford, *Of Plymouth Plantation*, ed. Samuel Eliot Morison (New York, 1952), 86.

decide that the contract of marriage could dispense with *all* intermediaries, that it need involve no one but the two essential parties themselves. The General Court at Plymouth watched carefully to suppress this tendency whenever it appeared. Thus, for example, the Records show that in 1678 Edward Wanton was fined £10 for "disorderly joyning himselfe in marriage"; [45] and at least a few similar cases seem to have occurred both before and after this.[46] The code of 1671 stated the legal necessities very clearly: "no person in this Jurisdiction shall joyne any persons together in Marriage but the Magistrate, or such other as the Court shall authorize in such place where no Magistrate is near, nor shall any joyn themselves in Marriage, but before some Magistrate, or person authorized as aforesaid." [47] In fact, the Court had been appointing men to this responsibility (normally on the basis of one per town) for many years previous.[48]

It is thought that the bride's home was the usual place for a wedding ceremony, and that no set prescriptions defined its content. Apparently any fitting words would do, and perhaps the whole affair was characterized by a kind of rough and ready spontaneity. Some evidence exists from eighteenth-century Massachusetts to connect weddings with a certain type of feasting and celebration, but there is nothing comparable for seventeenth-century Plymouth.[49] Like so many other things in the Old Colony,

45. *Plymouth Colony Records*, V, 263.
46. *Plymouth Colony Records*, III, 46, 52 (case of Edward Perry); III, 206 (case of Robert Whetcombe); VI, 125 (case of William Gifford).
47. Brigham, *The Compact with the Charter and Laws of the Colony of New Plymouth*, 272.
48. For example, the following Court order of June 10, 1662: "The Court have authorised Mr Timothy Hatherly to sollemise the ordinance of marriage in the township of Scittuate as occation shall require, and likewise to adminnester an oath . . ." These orders are a faily standard item in the Records after about 1645.
49. The very meager evidence on seventeenth-century marriage ceremonies was assembled by Alice Morse Earle, in *Customs and Fashions in Old New England* (New York, 1894), 73 ff. See also Chilton L. Powell "Marriage in Early New England," *New England Quarterly*, I, 328; and Morgan, *The Puritan Family*, 33. It does seem likely that weddings in the Old Colony

weddings were probably short, simple, and very much to the point.

We must now turn to a very important question bearing on the lives of any couple in this community during the years after their marriage: how much, and for how long, did they remain beholden to their own parents? The issue has been raised in its most compelling form as a result of research on the early history of the town of Andover, Massachusetts;[50] but it could well be generalized to include other parts of New England in the seventeenth century—among them Plymouth Colony. Wills are particularly important to this research for the light they throw on certain aspects of the relationship between fathers and sons. They are said to imply that a man would normally retain title to all his lands until the time of his death, *including* those which he gave (in a limited sense) to his grown sons as "portions." This meant that many people did not become truly independent until they were well along into middle age. And it also meant that the aging father held a whip hand over his sons, in the form of the power to disinherit. Here, then—so it is argued—was the basis for a truly "patriarchal" system of authority.

Some of the wills from Plymouth can be fitted exactly to these specifications. Thus when John Gorham of Yarmouth died in 1678 he directed that his eldest son should "have the Dwelling house that hee now lives in, with the barne and halfe the upland belong-

---

were the occasion for a gathering of friends and family, and that some sort of food and drink was enjoyed afterwards. Emmanuel Altham, one of the earliest visitors to the Colony, observed Governor Bradford's wedding in 1623, and wrote of certain "very good pastime"—that is, entertainment—provided by the local Indians. He also spoke of "twelve pasty venisons, besides others, pieces of roasted venison and other such good cheer . . ." (See *Three Visitors to Early Plymouth*, ed. Sidney V. James [Plymouth, 1963], 29.) But it is difficult to imagine that this was a typical ceremony.

50. See an important article by Philip J. Greven, "Family Structure in Seventeenth-Century Andover, Massachusetts," *William and Mary Quarterly*, 3d Ser., XXIII, 234-56. Mr. Greven's research on Andover is presented at greater length in his Ph.D. dissertation, *Four Generations*, deposited in the archives, Widener Library, Harvard University. (A revised version will be published shortly by Cornell University Press.)

ing to the said farme." [51] More commonly, perhaps, land alone
was involved: the house that the son had built was considered to
be his own, but the ground on which it rested remained the property of his father—pending a final conveyance by will. The usual
formula was roughly this: "I give unto my son, John Spooner,
that thirty acres of land where he now dwelleth." [52] Occasionally
it was spelled out in a little more detail: "And whereas I Gave
unto my son John half a share of land formerly And he hath
nothing to show for it I now Give it him by will and he shall
have fifty Acres of land where his house standeth." [53]

There is, moreover, at least one piece of evidence suggesting
that such nebulous arrangements could lead to considerable tension and conflict within a given family. It comes from a set of
legal proceedings relating to the final settlement of the estate of
Samuel Ryder in 1679. Ryder had recently died, leaving two sons
(Benjamin and John) as his chief heirs, while excluding a third
(Joseph) altogether. Yet some time previously Joseph had built a
house on a piece of his father's land, with the expectation of re-
ceiving formal title to it in the father's will. Now—obviously distressed—he set out to break the will, in an appeal to the General
Court. Two depositions from a couple named Mathews described
the specific events out of which the whole sequence of trouble
had developed.[54] From Elizabeth Mathews: "I being att the Raising of Joseph Riders house; Joseph Ryders Mother Came into the
house Joseph then lived in and Cryed and wrong her hands fearing that Joseph would Goe away; Josephs Mother then said
that if you would beleive a woman beleive mee that youer father
saith that you shall never be Molested; and you shall Never be

51. *Mayflower Descendant*, IV, 157. See also the wills of Samuel Wilbore
of Taunton (*Mayflower Descendant*, XIV, 150–51) and Ephraim Tinkham
of Plymouth (*Mayflower Descendant*, IV, 122–24).
52. Thomas Spooner, *Records of William Spooner of Plymouth, Mass.,
and His Descendants* (Cincinnati, 1883), 19.
53. Will of John Thompson of Middleborough, *Mayflower Descendant*,
IV, 23.
54. *Mayflower Descendant*, XI, 50–53.

Molested." From Samuel Mathews: "In the Morning before wee Raised the house old Goodman Ryder Joseph Ryders father Came out and marked out the Ground with his stick; and bid the said Joseph sett his house where it Now stands . . . the occation of the womans Lamenting as above said was fearing her son would Goe away; for shee said if hee went shee would Goe to."

So much for the evidence that seems to match the Andover pattern: unfortunately there are plenty of other indications—some of them ambiguous, some directly contrary. Certain wills, for example, simply report gifts of land and other property made long ago in the past. The will of Dolar Davis of Barnstable contains this clause—"I haveing alreddy Given my sons Symon and Samuell theire full portions and Deeds for theire lands which I have settled on them" [55]—by way of explaining the absence of any further bequests to these two. Similar considerations were behind the statement that Governor Thomas Hickley placed near the beginning of his own "last will & testament": "I have given to all my Children which are married there portions heretofore as farre as my low Estate would well bear." [56]

Still another group of wills—perhaps the most difficult of all to interpret with any sense of assurance—refers to gifts made previously and now (on the occasion of the father's death) "confirmed." In a typical case, the wording reads as follows: "Item: I have already Given unto my son Samuel and Do hereby Confirm unto him and his heires All the ffarme he now liveth on." [57] Occasionally it was a matter of confirming a previous confirmation: "I having already by Deed under my hand and Seal Dated the

---

55. *Mayflower Descendant*, XXIV, 71.
56. *Mayflower Descendant*, V, 239. See also the wills of Henry Andrews of Taunton (*Mayflower Descendant*, XI, 152–56), Myles Standish of Duxbury (*Mayflower Descendant*, III, 153–56), John Howland of Plymouth (*Mayflower Descendant*, II, 70–73), George Soule of Duxbury (*ibid.*, 81 ff.), John Soule of Duxbury (*Mayflower Descendant*, IV, 159), and Richard Wright of Plymouth (*ibid.*, 165).
57. Will of Benjamin Bartlett of Duxbury, in *Mayflower Descendant*, VI, 45.

19th day of August 1674 Given and Confirmed to my Eldest son Daniel White my Tenement or Homestead with other my land and Rights of Land in ye Township of Marshfield . . . —All which lands and premisses I hereby further Confirm unto him." [58] (Daniel White, incidentally, was married in the summer of 1674, and the gift mentioned here in his father's will must surely have been related to this event.) Sometimes the particular word "confirm" was omitted, but the general import seems to have been the same: "I Give to my Son Joseph The land whereupon he lives of which have already Given him Assurance by Written Deed"; [59] and "what estate I have formerly settled on my eldest son Kanelme . . . shall remaine unaltered." [60] (But would it, then, *ever* have been possible to alter a "settlement" arranged long before?)

Finally, there are at least a few wills which seem to represent two of these different patterns within the same individual compass. The instructions left by John Washburn, an unusually wealthy resident of Bridgewater, provide a good case in point. Consider these two separate clauses in his will: (1) "to my Son John Four-score acres of upland in the place where he hath already Built." (2) "to my Son Joseph I have Given twenty acres of land lying at Satucket pond. . . . I have otherwise Done for him according to my ability And my will is that he therewth Rest Contented." [61]

The wills are both numerous and obviously central to the problem we are considering, but certain other types of material should be investigated as well. There are, for example, the contracts drawn up at the time of a marriage. The wording of these docu-

---

58. Will of Peregrine White of Marshfield, in *Mayflower Descendant*, I, 130.
59. Will of Joseph Alden of Bridgewater, in *Mayflower Descendant*, VI, 72.
60. Will of Kenelm Winslow, in *Mayflower Descendant*, XXIV, 41.
61. *Mayflower Descendant*, XV, 248–49. See also the will of John Turner of Scituate, *Mayflower Descendant*, V, 41.

ments sounds quite unequivocal: the properties promised to the contracted couple will become theirs—without qualification. Thus in 1650 when Governor William Bradford conveyed a large farm near Plymouth to his son (who was about to be married) the deed was written as follows: "I Doe therefore by this my Graunt give Graunt and Confeirme and Rattifye [the property] . . . To him and his heires for ever." [62] The comparable clause in another of these deeds from a few years later reads: "I . . . Doe promise to give signe and sett over att prsent one third of all my lands to bee my son Josephths proper Right for ever; to him and his wifes for ever alsoe." [63] The same pattern can be viewed retrospectively in certain notations from the Records of the General Court. In 1675, while settling the estate of Mr. Josiah Winslow, the Court disregarded a clause in his will bequeathing "his house, and all his lands lying and being in Marshfield" to a son named Jonathan. Its reasoning was that Jonathan had been given these properties several years earlier "in franke marriage unto Ruth, the daughter of Mr William Serjeant," and "a man can not by his last will and testament defeat and make void a gift of lands made unto his son and heire in franke marriage." [64] Here, it seems, is firm *legal* evidence of the finality imputed to such contracts.

In some instances the conveyance of lands from father to son cannot be directly correlated with the start of a marriage. A deed of 1658 declared that John Dunham "hath freely and absolutely given and made over unto his son Jonathan Dunham . . . all that his house and land that the said Jonathan Dunham is Now Possessed of and liveth upon." [65] Jonathan Dunham was at this time twenty-six years old, but already on his second marriage. He had married first some three years earlier, had lost his wife almost immediately, and had then remarried. Now, a little belatedly perhaps but not radically so, he obtained his economic independence.

62. *Mayflower Descendant*, IX, 66.
63. *Mayflower Descendant*, XVI, 82.
64. *Plymouth Colony Records*, V, 159.
65. *Mayflower Descendant*, XII, 214.

On the other hand, John Browne of Rehoboth took steps in 1653 to "assigne give and bequeath unto my two sonnes viz John Browne and James Browne all my right title and enterest which I have into a prcell or tracts of land which this prsent Day I have bought of my sonneinlaw capt: Thomas Willet." [66] So far as can be learned, both sons were in their middle twenties, and *neither one* was married. Equally pertinent are the deeds through which George Robinson of Rehoboth conveyed some of his lands to his two sons, George Jr. and Samuel.[67] They bear the same date, July 14, 1681. George Jr. was then twenty-five years old and had been married a few months previously. His brother Samuel was twenty-seven, but as yet single; indeed he would not be married for another seven years.

This long compilation of data must now be ended and an effort made to assess its total meaning for the issue of "partriarchal" authority. Consider the following, by way of a summary: (1) The wills can be separated into several different categories. Some grant properties already possessed but not formally owned by the testator's children. Some confirm previous grants. And some merely report previous grants. It is impossible to measure these categories in any quantitative sense, but no one of them appears conspicuously larger than the others. Moreover, there are at least a few wills which seem to join *two* of these patterns together. (2) The grants made on the occasion of a marriage seem to provide for full and permanent ownership. (3) Similar grants were made without direct consideration of marriage; indeed in some cases they involved men who were both young *and* quite definitely single.

The picture is, then, at certain points ambiguous; but one result of a negative kind seems eminently clear. *There is little warrant in these materials for any general assumption that parents deployed*

66. *Mayflower Descendant*, IV, 84.
67. See Richard LeBaron Bowen, *Early Rehoboth* (Rehoboth, Mass., 1948), III, 164.

their ownership of property so as to maintain effective control over their grown children. In fact, it would be easier to argue the opposite case: that for most people a real and decisive measure of economic independence came rather early in their adult lives, and that if they remained at all beholden to their parents it was for reasons more psychological than material. But of these latter possibilities the evidence tells us nothing.

CHAPTER ELEVEN

LATER YEARS

It is extremely difficult to find a meaningful way of discussing the whole second half of life—the periods designated by our terms "middle age" and "old age"—from the developmental point of view. This is partly because the available materials do not seem very numerous, or at least not very revealing, and partly because we have little in the way of developmental theory to provide a framework of analysis and to help us single out the significant details. We have done our best to watch the colonists pass through childhood, to get them safely married and established in an autonomous, adult life; but now there is little more to say. Or, to put it another way, what *can* be said seems to comprise an obvious range of routine, everyday activities. Life is filled with business and family affairs—with buying and selling land, raising children, presiding over a household, joining neighbors in various civic projects (or competing with them for some tangible sign of wealth or prestige)—and yet at a deeper level, it seems to stand still. We lose the feeling not just of growth, but of change in any sense.

Is this a "true" picture of later life, theirs *or* ours? Or does it rather show a kind of shortsightedness, some flaw in the eye of the beholder? Was it indeed the view of the colonists themselves? Certainly there is nothing in the evidence they have left behind to suggest any important turning points, any more or less specific "boundaries" between one sort of experience and another, in the course of their lives after the attainment of maturity. Perhaps in individual cases there were changes of an internal sort—private sorrows, moments of personal triumph; but this would be difficult material for generalization, and it is in any case impossible to document.

One way alone remains for obtaining some notion of the basic instincts of the colonists about age—and aging; and it involves the matter of officeholding, of leadership. To what extent was age a factor in the selection of men to conduct the affairs of the community at large? Did the society seem to favor one age group over another in the distribution of power and prestige? Might the frontier environment, for example, have worked to improve the position of a relatively young man as against an older one?

Individual cases come to mind fairly easily, but unfortunately they can be found on either side of the issue. William Bradford assumed the governorship of the Colony at the age of thirty-one. John Howland and John Dunham both served the town of Plymouth as Deputies to the General Court when they were well along in their seventies. John Alden became an Assistant at thirty-three—but was still being regularly re-elected to that post fifty years later. About all such data tell us is that age was not the *only* factor affecting the choice of men for leadership, that neither the young nor the elderly had an exclusive claim on this kind of preferment.

It seems wiser therefore to try to think in terms of averages, of broad regularities—with the aim of reaching a level of implicit assumption and belief which is none the less important for being quite diffuse. To this end let us examine the results of a relatively simple probe designed to discover the ages of the men who served in various parts of the Colony's government. Consider first, the Governors and their Assistants, as sampled at six different points in time: 1635, 1645, 1655, 1665, 1675, 1685. In each instance this represents a total of eight persons (a Governor and seven Assistants), save in the last where there are seven (a Governor, a Deputy-Governor, and five Assistants). The average age of each group works out as follows: 44.0, 55.4, 61.6, 53.1, 58.0, 58.5. And the average for the whole sample is 55.0.

But another question immediately suggests itself: how broadly do the individual cases spread out on either side of the average? To find an answer the total of 47 cases must be broken down into separate age groupings. Three of them were in their thirties, thirteen in their forties, thirteen in their fifties, eleven in their sixties, five in their seventies, and two in their eighties. In short, there is a fairly even distribution between the ages of forty and sixty-nine, but relatively few cases outside this range (just over 20 per cent of the whole). Still another way of approaching the problem is to examine the age at which men *first* came to the office of Governor or Assistant. Briefly: the average here is 45.4 years, with nearly half the sample falling into the forties' category.

Similar techniques can be employed with samples of Deputies and selectmen. Take, for instance, the Deputies from the town of Plymouth, at ten-year intervals from 1640 to 1690. This comes to a total of 18 cases, and produces an average of 50.7 years. And the average age of *first* service for such men is 43.7. Plymouth did not choose selectmen until 1666, so in order to have several groups to investigate the intervals in time must be reduced to five years (1666, 1671, and so forth, through 1691). This procedure yields 19 cases and an average of 54.3 years, Finally, the average age of first service for the selectmen of Plymouth comes to 43.9.

It is striking to find such a uniform set of figures covering the different offices under consideration. And this uniformity does imply certain fundamental assumptions about the relation between age and responsibility which may now be summarized. The Old Colony was not, in the first place, a community which conferred an unusual degree of power and position on youth. In the normal life sequence significant responsibilities might come only after the age of forty. A man would have ten or fifteen years of experience as an independent householder before being called to office; and this was true in equal measure of positions at both the local and the whole-Colony level. Exceptions there were: really unusual qualifications in terms of family background, wealth, or demonstrable character strength might serve to advance the timetable. But for present purposes the average man, or rather the average office-holder, is the crucial datum. Moreover, at any given time the major governing units of the Colony would contain a preponderance of men of "middle age" or older. The average was likely to fall somewhere between fifty and sixty. It may be noted, in passing, that this pattern seems remarkably similar to what usually obtains in our own day. Presidents, Cabinet members, Congressmen, and a variety of local officials tend also to be distributed along an age range from forty to seventy. Indeed if the figures were to be worked out in detail, the average might well prove lower today than it was three centuries ago at Plymouth.

Let us shift our attention now so as to focus more directly on the closing phase of a man's life—the years, say, after sixty-five. The material on officeholders makes one point immediately apparent: the colonists had little idea of retirement—little, that is, beyond a retirement that was made necessary by illness or extreme infirmity. The Assistants, for example, seem only rarely to have left their posts of their own accord, nor were they often voted out of office by their constituents. Usually their tenure was ended by death, which in some instances was very long delayed. Alden set a record that would never be surpassed when he died in harness at eighty-seven, but others were not so far behind. Of the Colony's six Governors, Carver, Bradford, Prence, and Josiah Winslow all died in office. (A fifth, Edward Winslow, served only two brief terms and subsequently returned to England; and the last one, Thomas Hinckley, was still going strong at seventy-three when Plymouth merged with Massachusetts Bay.)

Personal data of this kind can be amassed with very little effort. Myles Standish was continuously at the head of the Colony's military establishment from the time of settlement until his death in 1656 at the age of seventy-two. In 1659 the General Court directed that an aide be found for William Collier, a longtime Assistant. Collier was seventy-five at the time and was thought to need help because of "age and much business." [1] The possibility that Collier might leave the government, or cut back on the "much business," seems not to have figured in the Court's deliberations; instead its aim was to work out a satisfactory adjustment between the various demands and pressures on the old man. A generation later James Cudworth was acting a similar part. After having served for more than two decades as an Assistant, Cudworth in 1680 accepted a mission to England, to plead for the Colony in the delicate political negotiations then in progress. From our vantage point this sounds like quite an undertaking—for a man of seventy-six! Cudworth survived the long ocean voyage without difficulty, only to contract smallpox and die within days of his arrival.

It is easier to measure these careers in public service than to find comparable materials bearing on the *private* pursuits of elderly men. But almost certainly the same basic assumptions prevailed. Samuel Eddy, for example, apparently continued his work as a tailor until quite an advanced age; for in 1678, when he was over seventy, the Court was approving money to reimburse him for helping to outfit the Colony's soldiers in King Philip's War.[2] More generally, many of the wills written by elderly men imply a direct and exclusive interest in the continuing management of their farms: there would be no change in this situation until the

1. *Plymouth Colony Records*, III, 166.
2. *Records of the Town of Plymouth*, I, 151.

moment of the testator's death. We did note earlier certain cases in which the testator mentioned some particular assistance provided by a child or other relative. But they seem on their own evidence to have been regarded as somewhat exceptional. Often there is explicit reference to the "extreme old age and weakness" of the one party—by way of explaining the need for the solicitude of the other. Clearly similar was the case of the man who conveyed his property to someone else *before* death in exchange for a guarantee of personal care. The reason for such arrangements was presumably the one mentioned by Samuel Nash (see above, p. 76): "being aged, and not in a capassety to live and keep house of himselfe." [3] Conversely, so long as the "capassety" remained, a man would prefer to hold direct control over his property, and direct responsibility for the day-by-day management of his affairs.

Insofar, as the culture did propose to distinguish the elderly from the rest of the populace, it emphasized "their long experience, and manifold advantages . . . for the getting of wisdom." [4] The approved role for the old man was the dispensing of "counsel" to others, particularly the young. He should, as a consequence, be treated more respectfully; indeed "a bashful and modest reverence" was his due under virtually all conceivable circumstances.

But this sort of stereotype is not worth elaborating in any great detail, since it is still familiar enough today. Rather more important, perhaps, is the whole question of actual *behavior* in this regard. No comprehensive answer can be given, but there are at least some scraps of evidence to suggest that old age brought its own share of difficulties, and its own particular worries, for many people in the Old Colony. Elderly men, for example, seem to have been no less immune to suits or other actions at Court than anyone else. And some of these episodes revealed a deep strain of bitterness that was not muffled by any sense of discrepancy between

3. *Plymouth Colony Records*, VI, 125–26.
4. *The Works of John Robinson*, I, 253.

the ages of the people involved. Consider the following piece of testimony in a case at Scituate in 1685. The chief participants are Nathaniel Parker, age twenty-three, and Edward Jenkins, age approximately sixty-five; the setting is Jenkins's house; and the issue between them is a debt of several "bolts" of cloth. Parker (as the debtor) declared that "he had noo boults at present without he should stele them for him and that he wold not doo: as sum had dun . . . as soon as nathanell parker had spook these words: edward jenkins tould nathanell parker that hee never brook up elder kings chest and took mony out of it with that nathanell parker ran too edward jenkins and [took] edward jenkins by the color or the neckcloth that was about edward jenkins neck and nathanell parker . . . sayed god dame me if thou wart not a ould man I wold bet they teeth douen thy throt."⁵ It seems from this testimony that the two men confronted each other on a footing of equality—if, indeed, Parker's last comment is not meant to express contempt for his adversary's weakness as an "ould man." Certainly it is quite an uninhibited performance on both sides.

Worst of all, perhaps, for most elderly people was a nagging fear of being ignored or abandoned by those who should be closest to them. This fear shows up in some of the wills already quoted—in the elaborate efforts, for instance, of a dying man to ensure that the needs of his widow will be fully met (see above, pp. 75–76). Occasionally these arrangements did not work out. When William Clark of Duxbury died in 1687 he willed his entire estate to "william bonny (whom I brought up from his Childhood),"

5. Ms. deposition in the "Davis Scrapbooks," III, 8, at Pilgrim Hall, Plymouth Mass. This quotation is unusually rough and complicated, and may warrant some sort of "translation" into modern usage. With only spelling and punctuation changed it would read: "he had no bolts at present without he should steal them for him, and that he would not do, as some had done. . . . As soon as Nathaniel Parker had spoken these words, Edward Jenkins told Nathaniel Parker that he never broke up Elder King's chest and took money out of it. With that Nathaniel Parker ran to Edward Jenkins and took Edward Jenkins by the collar or the neckcloth that was about Edward Jenkins's neck, and Nathaniel Parker . . . . said 'God damn me, if thou were not an old man I would bat they teeth down thy throat.'"

provided that Bonny would continue to live in his house and look after his aged widow Martha. But scarcely more than a year later Martha Clark complained to the Court that Bonny had left her, and a warrant was issued for his arrest. He was duly apprehended and the will was read to him in the presence of a magistrate. But "he Answered that he would Rather than goe to dwell with her again Renounce his legacy." [6] Certainly this was *not* a typical occurrence: in the great majority of cases the aged and infirm received whatever care they required from their children (or other kin, or servants). Yet in a land so open and a society so strongly marked by geographical movement, nothing was absolutely assured. There was always the chance that an elderly couple would at a critical moment find itself cut off from any ready source of help—with children settled elsewhere and perhaps not even in touch. A vivid metaphor from Bradford's history provides a final flourish for this picture. Bradford has been describing the whole process of dispersion which removed from the town of Plymouth so many of its finest citizens. But the image he chooses to express his sorrow about this process comes from another, much more personal dimension of experience. The town, he writes, was "like an ancient mother grown old and forsaken of her children, though not in their affections yet in regard of their bodily presence and personal helpfulness; her ancient members being most of them worn away by death, and these of later time being like children translated into other families, and she like a widow left only to trust in God. Thus, she that had made many rich became herself poor." [7]

6. *Pilgrim Notes and Queries*, IV, 4.
7. Bradford, *Of Plymouth Plantation*, 334.

CONCLUSION: THE FAMILY IN COMPARATIVE PERSPECTIVE

The relationship between the inner workings of the family and the larger historical process is extremely intricate. Few scholars have attempted to chart its course through time—to discover, that is, at what rate and for what reasons changes in the one sphere have significant effects in the other.[1] Of course, no such effort is feasible here. Still it may be useful to attempt a brief comparative review of the family then and now, if only as a means of pulling together the various materials from Plymouth.

It seems, in the first place, that the whole area of membership and underlying structure presents some striking instances of conti-

1. Two studies which *do* propose some important ideas in this connection must be cited here: Bernard Bailyn, *Education in the Forming of American Society* (Chapel Hill, N.C., 1960), and Talcott Parsons and Robert F. Bales, *Family, Socialization, and Interaction Process* (Glencoe, Ill., 1960). The brilliant essay in "hypothetical history" which forms the first part of Bailyn's book is really as much about the family as about education; my own substantial indebtedness to it should be obvious. The work of Parsons and Bales, while suspect in its rendering of certain historical details, provides a most useful theoretical framework for understanding the relation of the family to society at large.

nuity. From the very beginning of settlement at Plymouth the family was nuclear in its basic composition and it has not changed in this respect ever since. One adult couple and their own children formed the core of each household—with the addition in some cases of an aged grandparent or "servant." Only the latter term introduces a real element of difference from the pattern of our own day. Insofar as it designated children purposely "bound out" from some other family, it stands in some degree to confound us. Also (though less often) included among the servants were orphans and certain types of deviant or sick persons. But aside from this the typical domestic unit is easily recognized in our own terms. Moreover, the settlers' definition of kindred (beyond the immediate family), and the range of effective contacts between such people, seem equally similar.

Of course, families were considerably larger in the seventeenth century than they are today. And this difference is magnified by the further differences in typical house plans. Most Old Colony dwellings were extremely small by our own standards, and even so parts of them were not usable during the long winter months. Thus there was little privacy for the residents, and little chance to differentiate between various portions of living space. Life in these households was much less segmented, in a formal sense, than it usually is for us; individuals were more constantly together and their activities meshed and overlapped at many points.

Still, despite this rather different set of physical arrangements, the usual alignment of roles and responsibilities within the family was basically similar to the modern American pattern. The husband was head of the household, and, at least in theory, the final arbiter of its affairs. Yet the wife had her own sphere of competence and a corresponding measure of authority. In certain most important areas of family life—the sale of real property or the disposition of children—the couple would make decisions *together*.

Possibly the lines of authority between parent and child were much tighter and more formal than in our own society; but the evidence on this point is not conclusive. In any case, the experience of childhood and growth through time did follow a course more distinctively its own. Childhood as we know it did not last much beyond the age of six or seven years. After that, participation in adult activities began in earnest. There was little schooling of the kind—the institutional kind—which in our own day helps to set apart a very broad age group. Instead children spent most of their time working (and relaxing) alongside older people, and were generally perceived as "little adults." If six or seven marked a turning point of greater import in the seventeenth than in the twentieth century, the opposite was true of adolescence. At Plymouth the "teens" formed a period of relatively calm and steady progress toward full maturity. Courtships began at this stage; and, though officially restricted by requirements of parental approval, they seem in many respects to have followed the lines of personal inclination. Marriage came somewhat later than it does now and needed at the outset substantial gifts of property from both sets of parents. But such gifts were never withheld, and were often framed so as to establish the complete autonomy of the recipients. The later years of life in Plymouth Colony brought, in most cases, no new departures of a major kind. The process of managing a family, and tending an estate, provided an essential continuity. Positions of power and prestige came chiefly to those over forty, and might indeed be retained to a very advanced age. Most men yielded reluctantly to "old age" proper, "retiring" only when forced to do so by real infirmity.

The foregoing survey has focused chiefly on issues and trends internal to the family. But it is also important to consider the whole field of relationships joining the family with the community at large. And in doing so we reach at last an area where the contrasts between the Plymouth pattern and our own are far more striking than the continuities.

Consider, for a start, the range of *functions*—material, psychological, social, and otherwise—performed by the family then and now. Of course, there is an underlying core common to both sides of the comparison, and indeed to virtually all systems of family life. It comprises the fulfillment of certain basic and universal needs—most obviously, those for shelter, food, and sexual release. But beyond this lies a great variety of other possibilities—a vast territory of social purpose and activity in which the family may or may not be involved. And, broadly speaking, the history of the family in America has been a history of contraction and withdrawal; its central theme is the gradual surrender to other institutions of functions that once lay very much within the realm of family responsibility. Plymouth Colony, as much as any place, marks the beginning of this story. The point is implicit in much of our previous discussion, but it must now be brought directly to center stage.

The Old Colony family was, first of all, a "business"—an absolutely central agency of economic production and exchange. Each household was more or less self-sufficient; and its various members were inextricably united in the work of providing for their fundamental material wants. Work, indeed, was a wholly natural extension of family life and merged imperceptibly with all of its other activities.

The family was also a "school." "Parents and masters" were charged by law to attend to the education of all the children in their immediate care—"at least to be able duely to read the Scriptures." Most people had little chance for any other sort of education, though "common schools" were just beginning to appear by the end of the Old Colony period.

The family was a "vocational institute." However deficient it may have been in transmitting the formal knowledge and skills associated with literacy, it clearly served to prepare its young for effective, independent performance in the larger economic system. For the great majority of persons—the majority who became farmers—the process was instinctive and almost unconscious. But it applied with equal force (and greater visibility) to the various trades and crafts of the time. The ordinary setting for an apprenticeship was, of course, a domestic one.

The family was a "church." To say this is not to slight the central importance of churches in the usual sense. Here, indeed, the family's role was partial and subsidiary. Nonetheless the obligation of "family worship" seems to have been widely assumed. Daily prayers and personal meditation formed an indispensable adjunct to the more formal devotions of a whole community.

The family was a "house of correction." Idle and even criminal persons were "sentenced" by the Court to live as servants in the families of more reputable citizens. The household seemed a natural setting both for imposing discipline and for encouraging some degree of character reformation.

The family was a "welfare institution"; in fact, it provided several different kinds of welfare service. It was occasionally a "hospital"—at least insofar as certain men thought to have special medical knowledge would receive sick persons into their homes for day-to-day care and treatment. It was an "orphanage"—in that children whose parents had died were straightaway transferred into another household (often that of a relative). It was an "old people's home"—since the aged and infirm, no longer able to care for themselves, were usually incorporated into the households of their grown children. And it was a "poorhouse" too—for analogous, and obvious, reasons.

Since the entire community had an interest in the smooth performance of these various tasks, it seemed only natural that there should be a certain amount of direct governmental supervision over the family. When a given family failed in some area, or experienced serious conflict among its individual members, the authorities might decide to intervene. The "harmony" of husband and wife, the subordination of children to parents—even such internal matters as these came, in theory, under official scrutiny. The government was also empowered to determine *who* might head a household in the first place.[2] Undesirables could, if necessary, be warned away.[3] One quite early statute ordered that "no servant comeing out of England or elsewhere . . . be admitted his freedome or to be for himself untill he have served forth his tyme either with his master or some other although he shall buy out his tyme, except he have beene a housekeeper or master of a famyly or meete and fitt to bee so."[4] A contract of servitude was not, in short, simply a business arrangement, in which the servant might substitute cash for labor in order to obtain immediate freedom. It was also a kind of apprenticeship in householding: a young man would learn how to be head of a family by living in one for a time. The sole exception to these provisions was—quite logically—the servant who had previously been a head-of-household ("or meete and fitt to bee so").

The very different situation of the modern family requires no such extended review. But clearly most of the functions enumerated above have long since been transferred out of the family—transferred to other institutions specially contrived for the purpose. One could say, therefore, that the family now occupies far less social "space," that profound environmental pressures have

2. In 1636 the Court ordered "that none be allowed to be housekeeps, or build any cottags, till such time as they be allowed and approved by the Govr & Cowncell." *Records of the Colony of New Plymouth, in New England,* ed. Nathaniel B. Shurtleff and David Pulsifer (Boston, 1855–61), I, 44. The procedures for securing such approval were slightly altered as time went on, but the principle remained the same. Occasionally one sees it operating in a specific case—for example, in the following entry in the Court Orders of April, 1638: "Willm Maycumber, of Dorchester, coop, is lycensed to dwell wthin this govment, at Plymouth or elsewhere, upon the testymony of his good behavior hee hath brought wth him." *Ibid.,* 82.
3. In 1668 at a town meeting in Plymouth "it was . . . agreed that John Everson be forthwith warned to depart the towne with all Convenient speed." *Records of the Town of Plymouth* (Plymouth, 1889), I 106. For the record of a similar case at Marshfield, see Lysander S. Richards, *History of Marshfield* (Plymouth, Mass., 1901), 82.
4. William Brigham, *The Compact with the Charter and Laws of the Colony of New Plymouth* (Boston, 1836), 65.

worked relentlessly to reduce its importance in the overall scheme of things.

And yet the situation has another side as well. For while the family is now less important from a social standpoint, it may well be *more* important from a psychological one. The crucial factor here is a certain feeling of connectedness, or isolation, with regard to the community at large—the degree to which individual persons sense that their life in a family makes a natural whole with other aspects of their experience. At Plymouth, we have seen, the family was joined to other institutions and other purposes in an intricate web of interconnections. It did not stand out in any special way from adjacent parts of the social backdrop; it acquired no distinctive aura of emotional or ideological significance. Its importance, while impossible to doubt, was more assumed than understood—was, indeed, so basic and so automatic as to be almost invisible. Family and community, private and public life, formed part of the same moral equation. The one supported the other, and they became in a sense indistinguishable.

The point becomes clearer when set in contrast to the situation that obtains in our own time. No longer can one feel such an essential continuity between the various spheres of experience; the central threads in the invisible web have been broken. Partial connections unquestionably remain, but they seem conspicuous on that very account. And in some overall reckoning elements of disjunction and even of opposition loom largest by far.

The family, in particular, stands quite apart from most other aspects of life. We have come to assume that whenever a man leaves his home "to go out into the world" he crosses a very critical boundary. Different rules, different values, different feelings apply on either side, and any failure to appreciate this brings, inevitably, the most painful kind of personal distress. The contrast has, of course, a pejorative character. The family becomes a kind of shrine for upholding and exemplifying all of the softer virtues—love, generosity, tenderness, altruism, harmony, repose. The world at large presents a much more sinister aspect. Impersonal, chaotic, unpredictable, often characterized by strife and sometimes by outright malignity, it requires of a man that he be constantly "on his guard." It goads and challenges him at every point, and occasionally provokes responses of a truly creative sort; but it also exhausts him. So it is that he must retreat periodically within the family circle, in order to rest and to marshal his energies for still another round. In this instance the family is important not so much as the foundation for an ideal social order, but as the foil to an actual state of social disorder. It forms a bulwark against the outside world—destroy it, and anarchy reigns everywhere. It forms, too, a bulwark against anxieties of the deepest and most personal kind. For we find in the family, as nowhere else in our "open society," an indispensable type of protection against the sense of utter isolation and helplessness. Given all these circumstances family life is bound to seem somewhat more intense, more contrived, and far more self-conscious.

The source of these changes between the seventeenth century and our own is to some extent implicit in the foregoing discussion. The biggest single factor seems to have been the separation of work from the individual household, in connection with the growth of an urban, industrial system. This it was that gave profound meaning to the sense of an "outside" or "public" world. But in the American setting there was the added factor of mobility, geographical *and* social—all the competitive pressures generated by an expansive and democratic social order. Men had reason to feel somewhat anxious and insecure in the world of work: here, indeed, was the price they paid for the chance to better themselves—a whole darker side of "the American experiment." The family, meanwhile, was increasingly set off; and it was also invested with that special sort of moral halo which it still retains.

The crucial phase of this process lay within the nineteenth century and cannot therefore have any substantial place in the current study. But were there no omens, no glimmerings of what lay

ahead, in the experience of seventeenth-century families—and specifically, those of Plymouth Colony? Can we find in any of the
materials examined above a hint of the transformation the American family would later undergo? Or to put the question another
way: can we discover any point of stress or conflict between the
family system which the settlers brought with them from the Old
World and the environment which they found in the New? The
evidence is, as always, quite incomplete; but it does contain some
tantalizing and provocative clues. These clues, when arranged together, serve to focus attention on one particular quadrant of
Old Colony life: opportunity, mobility, expansion, and all the
concomitant effects on the thoughts and actions of a great number
of individual settlers.

There was, in the first place, the important factor of empty
land—the appearance, at least, of a whole continent awaiting settlement. We cannot recover all of the innermost feelings of the
colonists as they faced this prospect, but it does seem likely that
certain rather basic hopes and ambitions were powerfully stimu-
lated. As noted earlier, there is much material from Plymouth
suggesting a pervasive tendency to expand and to scatter—a tendency that the leaders of the Colony sought unsuccessfully to re-
strain. If the colonists' most deeply cherished ideals of community
life yielded so readily to these expansive pressures, can the family
have come through unscathed? Was there some analogous kind of
"loosening" in this respect as well? Of course, in a broad sense
dispersion attacked the notion of community head on—by definition, as it were; whereas families were transportable. And, in fact,
the migration within the Colony was not the kind that split large
numbers of families apart; in many cases complete nuclear units
were centrally involved. Yet there was, most likely, a more subtle
sort of corrosive effect. In the long run mobility was bound to
weaken somewhat the lines of authority around which the traditional family was structured.

Many individual pieces of evidence, cited in previous chapters, imply as much. Recall, for example, the testimony given in the case of the contested will of Samuel Ryder. Much of it concerned a time some years earlier when Ryder's son Joseph had proposed to "Goe away" if the father would not guarantee him title to a certain tract of land. The tension which suffused the whole episode was particularly apparent in the mother's intervention—her tearful plea to Joseph that "if hee went shee would Goe too." Who holds the powerful hand in this confrontation: the father with his control of the family land, or the son with his threat to move away? And should there have been any confrontation at all? Would such a thing have been as plausible in an Old World setting? Recall the *many* inheritances that were made conditional on the fulfillment by the recipient of some important filial obligations. Just how deeply did such conditions bite, in an environment which presented so many alternative (and perhaps more promising) opportunities? The Bradford metaphor of the "widow . . . grown old and forsaken of her children" gains additional meaning in this connection. And then, too, there is William Bonny telling the Court that he would rather "Renounce his legacy" than continue to live with his aged mistress, the widow Clark.

There is more that can be said—but only in a speculative way, since the relevant evidence has not survived. Very likely, the advantages of young people in terms of adaptability, sturdiness, and resourcefulness were particularly important, and *visible*, in frontier circumstances; and perhaps for this reason it was unusually difficult to maintain the traditional subjection of youth to age. Possibly the high premium on labor—any labor—worked gradually to improve the position of both children and women. The failure to sustain a tight pattern of community organization may also have exerted some influence here. The community, after all, acting through its constituted authorities, was supposed to serve as a kind of overseer of family life; but what would happen when its own integrity began to be compromised? The Colony Records contain a variety of official complaints that parents were neglecting their duties to their children, or that "yeong men" were spending too much time in "Inns and Alehouses." It is hard to know exactly how to interpret these statements, but they do suggest at least some degree of worry about the quality of family life.

Yet in the final analysis, we should beware of attributing too much importance to these hints of decline and decay. The family remained an absolutely central institution throughout the whole history of the Old Colony. Its power to withstand the challenge of a new physical setting and an increasingly fluid social structure is at least as impressive as the concessions it made. There is no reason to think that a young man, undertaking a move to a new settlement, found it easy to break contact with his own family of origin. Moreover, it is striking that when such a man reached his destination he joined with others of a like mind to establish a community on the same demographic and emotional foundations which he had known in the place of his childhood. The basic arrangements of family life, and its importance as well, were little altered in the newer towns.

The situation is, then, best understood in terms of ambivalence and conflict and a whole host of counter-tendencies that yielded no clear sense of direction, except perhaps in the very long run. In this sense, the story of the family forms only a part, albeit an important one, of the larger drama of early American history—the drama that lays bare the whole momentous process of interaction between the inherited traditions, values, and institutions which the first waves of settlers brought with them and the coercive pressures of a new and radically different environment.

APPENDIX

DEMOGRAPHIC TABLES

Table I

SIZE OF FAMILIES IN PLYMOUTH COLONY

	Average Number of Children Born	Average Number Lived to Age 21	Size of Sample
First-Generation Families	7.8	7.2	16
Second-Generation Families	8.6	7.5	47
Third-Generation Families	9.3	7.9	33

Note: The ninety-six families in this sample were chosen for analysis because the evidence on their membership seemed especially complete and reliable. Also, in all these families both parents lived at least to age fifty, or else, if one parent died, the other quickly remarried. Thus in all cases there were parents who lived up to, and past, the prime years for childbearing.

Table II

LIFE EXPECTANCY IN PLYMOUTH COLONY

Age	Men	Women
21	69.2	62.4
30	70.0	64.7
40	71.2	69.7
50	73.7	73.4
60	76.3	76.8
70	79.9	80.7
80	85.1	86.7

Note: The figures in the left-hand column are the control points, that is, a twenty-one-year-old man might expect to live to age 69.2, a thirty-year-old to 70.0, and so forth. The sample on which this table is based comprises a total of 645 persons.

Table III

DEATHS ARRANGED ACCORDING TO AGE (PLYMOUTH COLONY)

Age Group	Men (percentages)	Women (percentages)
22–29	1.6	5.9
30–39	3.6	12.0
40–49	7.8	12.0
50–59	10.2	10.9
60–69	18.0	14.9
70–79	30.5	20.7
80–89	22.4	16.0
90 or over	5.9	7.6

Note: The figures in columns two and three represent the percentages of the men and women in the sample who died between the ages indicated in column one. The sample is the same as in Table II.

Table IV

FIRST MARRIAGES IN PLYMOUTH COLONY

	Born Before 1600	Born 1600–25	Born 1625–50	Born 1650–75	Born 1675–1700
Mean age of men at time of first marriage	27.0	27.0	26.1	25.4	24.6
Mean age of women at time of first marriage	—	20.6	20.2	21.3	22.3
Percentage of men married at age 23 or under	25	18	25	26	38
Percentage of men married at age 30 or over	44	23	27	18	14
Percentage of women married at age 25 or over	—	9	10	20	28

Note: The sample on which this table is based comprises a total of 650 persons. There is, however, insufficient data for women born before 1600.

Table V

RATES OF REMARRIAGE IN PLYMOUTH COLONY

Number of Marriages	Men (percentages)		Women (percentages)	
	Over 50	Over 70	Over 50	Over 70
1	60	55	74	69
2	34	36	25	30
3	6	8	1	1
4	*	·5	—	—
5	*	·5	—	—
Total married more than once	40	45	26	31

Note: The sample on which this table is based comprises 711 persons. The asterisks indicate a figure of less than one-half of one per cent.

Table VI

SIZE OF HOUSEHOLDS (BRISTOL CENSUS, 1689)

Number of Persons in Household	1	2	3	4	5	6	7	8	9	10	11	12	13	14	15
Number of Families	1	6	5	11	9	13	5	7	6	3	2	1	0	0	1

Table VII

CHILDREN PER FAMILY (BRISTOL CENSUS, 1689)

Number of Children in Family	0	1	2	3	4	5	6	7	8	9	10
Number of Families	7	10	11	12	9	8	6	4	1	0	1

Table VIII

SERVANTS PER FAMILY (BRISTOL CENSUS, 1689)

Number of Servants	0	1	2	3	4	8	11
Number of Families	48	8	8	3	1	1	1

INDEX